JA

TY DETMER

THE MAKING OF A LEGEND

TY DETMER

THE MAKING OF A LEGEND

BY DICK HARMON

FOREWORD BY — HAYDEN FRY ★ ★ ★ INTRODUCTION — SONNY DETMER

Cedar
Fort

Back cover photograph by Pat Krohn

Published and Distributed by:

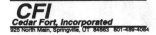

CFI
Cedar Fort, Incorporated
925 North Main, Springville, UT 84663   801-489-7084

Printed in the United States of Ameica

96 95 94 93 92   6 5 4 3 2

Library of Congress Catalog Card Number: 92-81910
ISBN: 1-55517-085-4

Cover Art by Scott Snow

Dedication

This book is dedicated to the remembrance of Hubert Detmer, Clyde Spellman, my son Jeffrey and my older brother Ron. Of these, only Hubert lived to see Ty Detmer play college football.

ACKNOWLEDGMENTS

This book could not have been written without the cooperation of many people who have come through with timely information, interviews, observations and counsel. I thank Ty Detmer for his patience with reporters, his standard of performance on and off the field and his gamesmanship. He is a rare human being. Obviously without the player there is no story. I thank Sonny and Betty Detmer for sharing their son with non-Texans. A special thanks is in order for the BYU coaching staff. I am grateful for the cooperation of head coach LaVell Edwards, who patiently and consistently grants writers access to his program through attendance at practice sessions, locker rooms and interviews with players and coaches. Edwards has always been an advocate of the media when he didn't have to. Without his cooperation the job of covering his football team would be tremendously difficult.

I would like to acknowledge the cooperation of the BYU sports information staff, particularly Val Hale and Ralph Zobell. I appreciate the encouragement of Stephanni Hicken, who put a gun to my head and made some deadlines. I thank Frances Smeath, whose bulldog editing skills are becoming legend.

No book would ever get out without a publisher, for which I thank Lyle Mortimer and his staff, especially Wendie Shumway, Jeff Lambson, Katherine Hatch and David Ingram.

I am in debt to Neil Reed, who is a walking encyclopedia. He has been with Ty from the beginning, recognizing his talent before anyone. Since my first conversation with Reed over six years ago on a live Provo radio show, everything he predicted about Ty Detmer has come true and the young All-American has never had a more devoted and loyal friend. If all parties involved in decision-making, college choices and playing time would have listened to Reed in 1985, Ty and Koy Detmer might have combined for 35,000 yards passing in their college careers and broken nearly every NCAA passing record.

My wife AnnaLee has provided emotional encouragement for this book for three years. I love and appreciate her and her faith in me. I also thank Brandon, Kylie and Courtney for giving me some breathing room while writing this work. I thank my brother Kent, and my parents, Rondo and June, for their technical and financial support. The work was accomplished during the busiest time of the season while I covered a bowl game and Western Athletic Conference basketball.

I owe a big thanks to a talented group of photographers; Mark Philbrick, Brian Tregaskis, Pat Krohn, Jason Olsen and David Dahl.

FOREWORD

Being a west Texas boy, I don't know if I could come up with enough adjectives to describe Ty Detmer. I don't have that kind of vocabulary. It comes from growing up in Odessa.

But being a Texan, I'm prejudiced for Texans and Ty Detmer is a Texan. He's as Texan as you can get. My great-great grandfather Benjamin Franklin Fry fought with Sam Houston and Ty Detmer's relatives against Santa Anna in the battle of San Jacinto. I know Ty's father Sonny and his brother Koy, a fine quarterback at Mission High. Ty comes from good stock and Texans take a lot of pride in their roots.

The Detmers are a football family. Sonny is one of the brilliant offensive minds in Texas. Ty set the Texas passing record while at Southwest in San Antonio and in 1991 Koy extended that record at Mission, becoming the state's all-time passing leader.

Ty may be the best college quarterback I've seen in 30 years as a college football coach. At the University of

Iowa we have had the Big 10 all-conference quarterback seven of the past nine years, including Chuck Long. We think we know something about evaluating quarterbacks and knowing their skill level and leadership. Ty is the best pure passer I've seen. He has tremendous leadership on the field and a presence that is commanding and demanding. He's one of the most inspirational leaders I've seen.

Ty has unbelievable radar. He knows when a guy is closing in on him from a rushing standpoint. He can elude him and then find his number three or four receiver down the field. Ty can throw back clear across the field when he's running full speed in one direction, find the guy and hit him right on the numbers.

Ty Detmer has got to be one of, if not the greatest quarterbacks to ever play college football. He sure ate up a lot of grass against us in the 1991 Holiday Bowl. Our team had been in the Rose Bowl the year before and that year we were the runner-up to Michigan in the Big 10. We were fortunate our defense kept BYU out of the end zone that night in San Diego and we tied 13-13. Still, Ty passed for 350 yards. That's a lot of real estate. At times in that game, Ty literally lifted that BYU offense and they followed him like a band does a drum major—they marched.

LaVell Edwards has had great quarterbacks at BYU over the years. They rank at the top of the NCAA record book in passing. Some of those quarterbacks who went before Ty threw a lot more passes in those earlier years. BYU had tried to be more balanced recently. I know LaVell Edwards has toughened up BYU's schedule the past five years and Ty's performances have been against improved competition. That tough competition adds even more credibility to what Ty has accomplished in his brilliant career.

Before we played against Ty, I stayed up late and watched that San Diego State-BYU game on TV; the one that ended in a 52-52 tie. Ty had suffered a cut over his eye and when he came off the field he'd put a towel over his eye and wipe the blood away. When it came time to go on the field, he'd throw down the towel, pick up his helmet and run on the field. He'd do that over and over. Ty showed he was a Texas football player. Boy, that guy has guts. When we played Ty in the Bowl game, he was everything we expected to see, a gutty playmaker and fierce competitor.

During that game I found myself watching Ty play and had to work at focusing my job of watching our defense. Ty is that kind of show.

Ty Detmer is a tribute to his family, his school and to the state of Texas. To be a football player in Texas is something special. It's a way of life for a boy to become a man and learn discipline, pride, develop teamwork, leadership, loyalty and courage. Ty Detmer embodies all of these things and I don't hesitate to represent Ty as an example for young people to follow.

This book, *Ty Detmer: The Making of a Legend,* by sportswriter Dick Harmon is a collector's item. This book examines Ty's background, his heritage and Texas roots. In this book Harmon has searched and found, and drawn comments from key, significant people who had a hand in Ty's development.

You don't need to take my word for what Ty has accomplished in throwing for more than 15,000 yards and winning the Heisman Trophy. Imagine throwing for nearly nine miles in a college career? I'm not sure if anybody will ever duplicate it. This book brims over with quotes and commentary from some of the great coaches in college football including Joe Paterno, Earl Bruce, Bobby Bowden and Terry Donahue. These men know football and they've played against Ty Detmer. This book also includes anecdotes and quotes from his junior high and high school coaches.

You'd want your son to be like Ty Detmer. You'd want your daughter to marry Ty Detmer. If you go to battle, you'd want Ty Detmer in your foxhole. If you play against him, he's not a player you want to take lightly, I promise you.

   —Coach Hayden Fry (Head Football Coach)
    University of Iowa
     May 1992

INTRODUCTION

Ty seems to always fall into things. He falls and walks into more stuff than I have ever run into in my life. Everything he does seems to work out. He has the golden touch.

One of the best things that ever happened to Ty was meeting up with the college sportswriter in Provo, Dick Harmon. We first got to know him the summer after Ty's junior year in high school. This was the summer Ty verbally committed to play for BYU. I guess Harmon routinely interviews BYU recruits. Harmon called our house to interview Ty and I live on a radio station. This evolved into a weekly Monday update on Ty's weekend games his entire senior year. When Ty or I couldn't come on the air with Dick Harmon, coach Neil Reed would give the Monday report.

We developed a friendship with Harmon and he became one of the first connections we had in Provo. Our family subscribed to *The Daily Herald* to read about BYU's football team. We were impressed with the day to day coverage of the team given by Harmon. He was objective and creative. He took an early interest in Ty and many of his columns and feature stories helped pave the way for Ty in Utah. People found out about him, they knew who he was, they discovered things about him, through Harmon, very early in his career. I know this opened a lot of doors for Ty. It wasn't long before Ty was no stranger in Utah. Our family credits that early interest in Ty to Dick Harmon.

There is only one writer who could have written this book—Dick Harmon, because he knows Ty. Dick Harmon has been on the sidelines and in the locker room covering Ty all the way, and that is important to this book. This book reflects Dick Harmon's first hand exposure to Ty and his background in Texas and BYU.

—Sonny Detmer
Mission, Texas
1992

TABLE OF CONTENTS

ONE

TEXAS FOOTBALL

Texas is a land of legends.

If ever these United States could claim a country within its boundaries, it would be Texas. This is a land adequately labeled with an asterisk, truly a Lone Star State. There is no place like Texas.

This is the land Texas Rangers once ruled. Hungry immigrants and cow-punching wranglers searched for fortunes, joined together in a drive for dreams of destiny. Texans love their heroes. The entire state is the quintessence of storied lore. Texans take pride in the fact that first governor Sam Houston refused to join the Southern States in seceding from the Union. Texans love recounting the battle of San Jacinto when Houston led Texans to victory over Santa Anna's Mexican Army. This avenged the Alamo, the death of Davy Crockett and the deaths of his spirited band of freedom fighters. Texas continually crowns the contradictions of its culture. It is the only state in the Union besides Vermont to have been an independent republic. Its people are stubborn, resourceful, rich and poor.

Texans are purists. Their love is simple. Their hate is clear. Their passion is perfect. A Texan sees life as a simple fight. The best man wins and the frail and weak fail. This is a land which brought the world the words of Woody Guthrie, the face of CBS-TV anchor Dan Rather, the laugh of Don Meredith, the ballads of Willie Nelson, and presidents Lyndon B. Johnson, Dwight Eisenhower and George Bush. In Texas none of those statesmen are as popular as Tom Landry, legendary coach of the Dallas Cowboys.

At the turn of the century, the horse-riding, cattle-driving cowboy symbolized the spirit of Texas. No one captured this spirit better than Larry McMurtry in his Pulitzer Prize-winning novel *Lonesome Dove*. McMurtry's characters carried on a symbolic struggle to conquer the dust bowl of the rugged Southwest.

In modern times the spirit of Texas is embodied in football, the state's unofficial religion. On Fridays, Saturdays and Sundays, gladiators of this faith don shoulder pads and helmets and enter temples made of concrete and steel. There the chants of worshippers ring in their ears as they sacrifice themselves for the glory of the game.

In Texas, football is bigger than life itself.

Only in Texas could there be America's Team, the Dallas Cowboys. The Dallas Cowboy Cheerleaders pioneered an entirely new sideline show copied by the sports world. Texas gave America Bum Phillips and Bum Bright. From the ranks of Texas high school came the inventor of the wishbone offense, Emory Bellard. The run-and-shoot offense found its root in the University of Houston, as did the popular veer offense.

Only in Texas could high school coaches have their own radio and television shows and get paid for speaking to booster groups the day before the game.

Only in Texas could high school football coaches serve as athletic directors, thus becoming administrators. They do not teach classes. This is the only state where football coaches negotiate their own contracts with school boards. They are the only personnel other than principals allowed that privilege. Few Texas high school coaches can afford the cut in pay to become college football assistants.

Only in Texas do school boards discuss whether their high schools should run or pass the football. They do it in open and closed executive sessions. In Texas, it is not uncommon for two schools to split gate receipts of $17,000 for a mid-season game. In Texas, season tickets to high school games are passed down from generation to generation. They are often included in wills and divorce decrees.

Only in Texas could a major college conference, the Southwest Conference, survive with universities exclusively within the geographic boundaries of one state. (With the departure of Arkansas in 1991 the SWC became a powerhouse comprised solely of Texas schools.) In Texas, college football got its first millionaire coach. That happened when Texas A&M

hired Jackie Sherrill away from the University of Pittsburgh, signing a multimillion-dollar contract and all the private Lear jets he could command. Only in Texas could the NCAA levy the most drastic penalty ever handed down to a college athletic program when Southern Methodist was sentenced to the "death penalty" (no football program of any kind) for NCAA violations in the late 1980s.

Only in Texas could a high school coaches' association of approximately 14,000 members become so powerful that candidates running for the state house and senate list the organization's name on campaign literature.

Only in Texas could spring football practice be the second biggest athletic event of the year, the first, of course, being the regular season. (As the Texans say, "There's football, and there's spring football!") Texas high schools pay all expenses for their coaches to fly anywhere in the United States to attend football camps and clinics. Athletic departments have the latest video electronic and weight training equipment.

Only in Texas could Texan George Bush become president of the United States and upon, receiving the Republican Party nomination, say in his acceptance speech: "And in time, we had six children; moved from the shotgun to a duplex apartment to a house, and lived the dream—high school football on Friday nights...."

How important is football in Texas?

4

Consider the words of Jim Norman, head coach at Big Sandy High School, as quoted by Jonathan Eisen and Harold Straughn in their entertaining book *Unknown Texas*:

"Nowadays I go to a football game and you know what I think about? Gladiators. I don't see a football game at all. I picture myself out there in a toga, and everybody's shouting, 'Kill the bum! Kill him!' Right here tonight you watch what happens. These fans go crazy. And yet, it's the one time in life for that hometown kid that he'll ever be known. He'll strut out there with that jersey and helmet on like a damn racehorse coming to run. The band's striking up and he's ready to go. God, it's the greatest thing in the world. He couldn't fight his way outta a wet popcorn bag, but I guarandamtee you right then he can whip anybody. His momma is up in the stands clapping and yelling for her boy, and soon as he gets a good lick he comes alimping off showing his battle scars. You ask that kid why he likes the game and he says, 'I don't know, just like it.' But it's so clear, so plain to see. We all want to be out there facing the challenge for our town, for our people. We'll never get that chance again. And if we get whipped five times in a row, we learn that you don't necessarily get whipped six. We learn to face the challenges one at a time. I mean that kid might get hit and rolled up like a nickel window shade. But he learns that if he keeps getting up he'll be admired, he'll be loved, he'll be a man, by god. It's something he may not get at home, and for sure not in the classroom."

Texas high schools are the hubs of their communities. Each local high school is a center of town pride. The best public facilities in a Texas town are at the schools. And at the schools, sports—particularly football—reign supreme. Temple High coach Bob McQueen explains:

"We take a lot of pride in our communities. Many of us are not far removed from our pioneer roots. Football is important in Texas because it is an opportunity for kids to stand up for their community. On Friday nights kids across the state stand at attention, their helmets off, hands over their hearts and listen to the national anthem. They learn to be gentlemen, to say 'no sir' and 'yes sir' and respect their teammates whether they be white or black. In the stands are their parents, neighbors. On the sidelines are 300 members of the band, drill teams and cheerleading squads. It involves everyone. Football teaches our youth discipline. It is easier to teach discipline on the football field than in the classroom or streets. Football is not only important, it is a necessary part of our lives."

San Antonio, Texas is a beautiful city. The San Antonio River meanders for nearly three miles through downtown. The Alamo, that enduring symbol of Texas independence, fortitude and pride, stands on East Houston Street. The River Walk, a network of cobblestone and flagstone paths, flanks the river. It is considered the jewel of the city and a feature many American cities have tried to copy. Tourists may take a river tour of San Antonio by boarding a barge near the Market Street Bridge every 10 minutes between 10 a.m. and 8 p.m. San Antonio is a city where Texas legends lived and died.

This is the city where schoolboy quarterback Ty Detmer became a legend.

Detmer is the first high school football player in San Antonio City history to win a Heisman Trophy. He became the eighth native Texan to win the coveted trophy that symbolizes the best college football player in America. The others include Andre Ware (Houston, 1989), Tim Brown (Notre Dame, 1987), Billy Sims (Oklahoma, 1978), Earl Campbell (Texas, 1977), John David Crow (Texas A&M, 1957), Doak Walker (Southern Methodist, 1948), and Davey O'Brien (Texas Christian, 1938).

In 1986, while only a junior at San Antonio's Southwest High School, Detmer was named the Texas High School Player of the Year. That year the bible of Lone Star State football, Dave Campbell's *Texas Football* magazine, ran a coverboy feature on Detmer. The headline read: "A Legend in the Making."

In the next six years Detmer became a three-time college All-American, Heisman winner, Maxwell Trophy National Player of the Year winner, the only two-time winner of the Davey O'Brien Memorial Trophy, and the recipient of the NCAA Top Six Award. In short, Detmer

7

is the most decorated football player in the history of Texas.

A legend?

The question is thrown to Pat Culpepper, head football coach at Lufkin, Texas. Culpepper earned All-America honors at the University of Texas back when players played both offense and defense. He was a member of the 1963 national championship Longhorn team. In short, Culpepper himself is a Texas legend. In his words:

"Ty Detmer is the perfect embodiment of Texas football. He is a fierce competitor, a leader, a player who displays courage and honor. Detmer led the way to revolutionizing Texas football with the passing game he learned from his father, Sonny. Ty has the heart of a lion and is as true a Texan as any defender of the Alamo. When he led BYU to a victory over Miami on national television, we saw a player wipe the blood from his chin and inspire his teammates. We saw a football player using his guts and his heart, picking himself off the turf and returning to battle.

"That day Texas football coaches across the state stood and said: 'By God, there is a Texan.'"

"Ty Detmer handled the ups and downs of his career with dignity and grace. He is a tribute to his parents, to his father, himself a Texas high school coach. He represents us all. Ty Detmer a legend? I would hope so."

TWO

IN THE SHADOWS OF THE ALAMO

Davy Crockett and Jim Bowie, heroes of the Alamo, were frontiersmen bred to become warriors. They became legends in the Texas Revolution of 1836. Crockett, a 10-year state representative from Tennessee, told his constituents to go to hell in 1835, and left his home for adventure in Texas. One year later he died defending the Alamo. Mexicans said Bowie had the blue eyes of a killer; they feared him more than any other white man. His use of a big knife became legend.

Ty Detmer came to San Antonio, Texas in 1968 as a one year old. Unlike Crockett, he didn't die within a year. Lufkin High School coach Pat Culpepper calls Ty Detmer a spirited football legend in the same mold as the heroes of the Alamo.

Ty Detmer is a seventh generation Texan. To be further linked to Texas, a person would have to be Comanche, Cherokee, Spaniard or Mexican. Ty's mother, Betty Spellman, can trace her ancestry back to what historians call the "Old 300." This was a group of settlers who came with Stephen F. Austin into Texas in the 1820s. These frontier families were given land grants from the ruling Spanish Commandant of Texas.

Later, Ty's distant cousins died fighting alongside the freedom fighters in the Alamo. Ty is a direct descendant of Zaddock Woods, one of the "Old 300" who built Woods Fort near St. Louis and housed such historic luminaries as Daniel Boone and U.S. president Zachary Taylor. Woods fought in the War of 1812 in the battle of New Orleans. Woods was in the mining business with Moses Austin, the father of Stephen. Woods and each of his four sons received Texas land grants and arrived in Texas Christmas Day in 1824. Zaddock Woods settled by West Point near La Grange on the Austin Highway. At age 70, Zaddock was killed along with 35 colonists by a Mexican garrison, September 18, 1842, in what is known as the Dawson Massacre. This was a skirmish leading up to the battle of the Alamo. That day Zaddock's son Gonzalvo escaped. His older son Norman was captured and taken deep into Mexico, where he died in Perote Prison in 1843.

In the confines of the Alamo, Crockett and Bowie gave their lives. In the shadow of that same monument Detmer created a life and legend of his own. Like Crockett and Bowie before him, he became an expert with a rifle, but his fame did not come with a gun.

Ty Detmer is a master of play. His gamesmanship and competitive spirit are legendary. Like rank and file fighters who followed Crockett and Bowie, Detmer's teammates came to love and admire the Texan. Ty Detmer, in a word, was fun. In the heat of battle his blood boiled. Away from the bright lights and pressure of a football game he hunted and fished. He pulled pranks. He kept practices alive with his dry humor. Sam Houston counted on Crockett, Bowie and Travis Buck to inspire courage in the face of battle. He didn't trust anyone else. BYU's coaching staff came to rely on Ty Detmer. They trusted him to deliver. He almost always did.

Ty Detmer could have been a star in a lot of sports. He grew up playing them all. He was a major league baseball prospect. But in baseball you only come up to bat once every two or three innings. He was a good shooter in basketball and played decent defense, but his potential in college was limited at six feet tall. So Ty Detmer chose his first love, football. He chose to be a quarterback, because he got his hands on the ball every single play.

People said Ty Detmer was too skinny, too small to excel as a quarterback. He proved them wrong. His whole life seems to be a test of proving he could play and win. After his sterling college career at BYU, some NFL experts said Ty would never make it as a professional. That made him even more determined. "I'll do it because they say I can't," he said.

When just a teenager, Ty won the coveted Muy Grande Big Buck contest in Texas by shooting the biggest deer. A 60-year-old man at the award ceremonies broke down in tears, happy he'd finished third. The old man had tried all his life.

In Utah, Detmer hunted and fished the mountains like Jim Bridger. With 20-15 vision and a velvet trigger hand, he could drop a deer with a shot through the heart from 600 yards. He would have been good against the army of Santa Anna. The Detmer apartment in Orem had a 30-year-old freezer in the middle of the living room. It was full of elk and deer meat.

Detmer kept his teammates off balance away from the field. He once stole the head of a pig at a luau and placed it in the bed of halfback Mike O'Brien. One Halloween he threw eggs at another teammate's apartment. He pelted the apartment with tomatoes inside and out. Inhabitants of the apartment had no idea who the culprit was. When a car came by for another pass, big defensive tackle Tim Adams raced to his car to chase the invading culprit. He grabbed a baseball bat on the way out. Adams was determined to end the pranks that night. He chased the car to a parking lot where he cornered the other vehicle. With his headlights shining on the suspect car, Adams got out with his bat. As he approached the car, he was shocked. "There was Ty," he said, "sitting there with this big goofy grin. We'd been had."

Detmer dominated in high school. The people in San Antonio never forgot Detmer. He dominated in college. The Utahns won't either.

"He controlled everything on the field," said former high school teammate Anthony Large, who worked at Lackland Air Force Base after high school. "I will never forget our opener in 1985, a 34-27 victory over 3A state champion Medina Valley. He really took control in that game. He got the team psyched up. If you didn't hold your block, he would kick you in the rear end. But after the game, he would come to you and say, 'Great game.' He was a leader. He was a coach on the field."

Another high school teammate, defensive lineman Kevin Lyssy, said Detmer's competitive spirit caught on to everyone who played with him. "He was the kind of guy you never expected to walk on the field and take over, but he was very much a dominating force."

Another lineman, John DeLuna agreed, adding, "He was always a calm type of person: level-headed and real smart. He just seemed to be in control all the time. He never lost his cool."

Ty Detmer was a Texan. He played like a Texan. He played like the heroes of the Alamo fought for freedom. He played to win and when he lost, it was not because he hadn't tried.

Like Crockett and Bowie, Detmer did not know the path to failure. He refused to walk off an athletic field with his tail between his legs. Ever. In 1991, his final year of college, playing UCLA in the Rose Bowl stadium in Pasadena, Ty faced another Texan quarterback in Bruin Tommy Maddox. After Maddox threw his second

13

interception of the game he got up slowly, holding his elbow as if injured.

On the sidelines Detmer screamed at the top of his lungs, "Quit acting like you're hurt. You're a Texan. We don't do that. You don't have an excuse. Act like a Texan, be a man."

Maddox stole a glance at Detmer. He understood.

The ghosts of Crockett and Bowie would have loved it.

That's what legends do.

THREE

THE PLAYMAKER

Penn State coach Joe Paterno labeled Ty Detmer a playmaker. That distinction differs from a player who runs plays. Florida State coach Bobby Bowden and veteran Iowa coach Hayden Fry agreed with Paterno that the most significant trait of quarterback Ty Detmer was his ability to milk a play for all it was worth. He was most dangerous when a play broke down and he improvised.

Ty Detmer has the ability to scramble and turn a disastrous lump of coal into a diamond. His father Sonny once claimed if somebody invented a game and gave Ty the rules, within a day Ty would master it and whip anybody. He'd do it at Nintendo or Tiddly Winks.

Ty's not only mentally swift, he's physically swift. In an interview in 1991, he responded to critics about his supposed weakness and slowness, in contrast to a player like former BYU quarterback and now '49er Steve Young, who can run 40 yards in 4.5 seconds. "I could go out on the practice field and run the 40 in 4.8 seconds (which is pretty slow) and people would question my speed," explained Ty. "But when in a game and the juice is flowing and guys are chasing me, I'd find myself running away from linebackers who run 4.5s."

San Diego State defensive coordinator Barry Lamb said Detmer was the best he'd ever seen at making something good out of something bad. "It's fun watching him on film. He really is a great playmaker and competitor. Game after game he eludes whatever rush there is, and he puts the ball right where it is supposed to be. You're not going to stop somebody like Ty Detmer. You try to slow him down and settle for that unless crazy things happen."

The fact never got much publicity, but Ty Detmer was a great baseball player. He even led the nation in hitting. It may be his best sport.

Just a few months after the Amarillo Chamber of Commerce named him the Texas Football Player of the Year in 1986, Ty found himself with bat in hand, at the plate, for the Southwest High Dragons. Southwest faced Edgewood High School in a game to determine the playoffs. The game with Edgewood centered in a region of Texas known for tough baseball. This region had produced Davey Johnson, Roger Hornsby, Roger Clemens, Nolan Ryan, Burt Hooton, Trisk Speaker, Eric Dickerson, Kyle Rote, Tommy Kramer, Thurmon Thomas, and Tommy Nobis.

Detmer came up to the plate that day as the best football player in the state of Texas, which is like Sir Lancelot's first appearance at King Arthur's court.

Everybody had their eyes on this skinny Dragon from Southwest; they wanted to see what made him tick.

While Ty was in the on-deck circle taking practice cuts, coach Neil Reed caught his attention and counseled, "Get ready. You're the Texas player of the year. Get ready to get down."

The Edgewood pitcher looked at Detmer, squinted at the catcher for a sign and began his windup. The first pitch came right for Ty's left ear; he ducked. Ty turned and smiled at Reed, who motioned to be careful. The second pitch came. Again it was a shot aimed right at Ty's head; he hit the dirt. Getting back up, he looked over at Reed. Ty flashed a grin.

The Edgewood pitcher had to throw a strike sooner or later because he wasn't about to walk Detmer and put Sir Lancelot on base. The third pitch came right down the gut. Ty, a doubles and triples line drive hitter like Don Mattingly, took the offering and crushed the baseball. It jumped off his bat as if shot out of a cannon. It sailed over the fence, clearing the trees which lined the park. It cruised over a house and floated across the street in front of a subdivision. Edgewood's players didn't move. They just watched the ball.

After the game Reed left the park and measured where the ball landed past the park fence. It was 470 feet. "It was a major league home run. Davey Johnson never hit it that far," said Reed with a laugh. Oh, yes. Southwest defeated Edgewood that day—the first sectional playoff victory for the Dragons in 34 years.

When Detmer was a sophomore, Southwest High's basketball team made the playoffs. Even in his early high school career Ty was a catalyst. In the first playoff game the Dragons played Laredo United, a powerhouse with a 28-2 record. In a tight game that went to the wire, players on Laredo's bench kept yelling for the team to foul Detmer, saying, "Foul the sophomore, foul the sophomore."

They did and Ty stepped up to the line and knocked down both free throws. Laredo would hit a bucket on the other end, then foul Ty, who'd plop down the charity tosses on the other end. Laredo would score and Ty would go swish, swish on the other end of the court. It seemed like one team against one player. Ty made nine free throws in a row that night. He didn't miss until the end of the game. Southwest won by one point. It was a night the Dragons needed a playmaker. They got one in Ty.

That same sophomore year, Southwest found itself getting thumped by the rich kids from Alamo Heights, a school set in an affluent San Antonio area. It was a game the Dragons had to win to make the playoffs. Southwest had a very talented team. They had height and speed. The Dragon team included 6-9 John Robertson, who went on to earn All Big West honors three years in a row at New Mexico State. Dragon Coach Mike Harris beat most of the 5A Top 20 teams in Texas while at Southwest. The Dragons were down 60-42 when Harris and his assistant, Neil Reed, told the

18

players they either had to kick dirt on the corpse and give up or fight for a win. Harris turned to Ty and a lightning-quick guard Maurice Brown, nicknamed "The Jet," and ordered a full court press.

With Ty and The Jet smothering Alamo Heights with ball-hawking pressure, the Dragons tied the game 62-all in two and a half minutes. Southwest won in overtime in a legendary victory.

The high school career of Ty Detmer is replete with examples of his athletic acumen, his playmaking ability.

His junior year, Southwest needed Ty to compete as a one-man team in the regional golf tournament. As the only Dragon, Ty went up against the country club boys from Alamo Heights, the annual Texas State golf champions. Although Ty hadn't picked up a golf club in months and certainly hadn't practiced the touch required for the short game, he used his booming 300-yard drives to outposition the field and led the competition for individual medalist honors after the first nine holes.

Off the field and court, Ty Detmer is a rather reserved, almost shy young man. He is polite almost to the book, listens well and has a hard time telling people no. He appears as a gentleman in every sense of the word and is known for his patience and long-suffering as well as his penchant for practical jokes and a dry sense of humor that can leave teammates straining from belly laughs.

But on the field of competition, Ty turns into a madman driven by a fire inside only winning fully quenches. He has that instinctive desire to compete, a drive that makes all the difference between running and sprinting. Detmer appears devoid of fear on a field of competition. Whether or not he actually is, it makes a big impact on teammates.

Practice sessions were never one of Ty Detmer's long suits. He just couldn't get all those coals inside heated up unless the game counted and people were after him. But practices with Ty Detmer were always fun. He'd always tease receivers when they'd miss easy passes; he'd pick on corner backs and have a laugh at them when they couldn't cover. He'd tease other quarterbacks who threw practice interceptions, although he threw some too. When a back would drop a screen pass, Ty would often mention the name of the star defensive player BYU would face that week and tell the back he must have been worried about that particular guy. Practicing with Ty Detmer was an experience, it was fun. One holiday season he showed up in long gray socks that only accentuated his skinny calves. Everyone laughed so hard the situation ruined the entire practice.

Bob Davis, one of the toughest middle linebackers to ever play at BYU, laughs remembering when he'd come up to the line and face Detmer, telling him he was going to kick his butt.

"Ty would look me right in the eyes, purse his lips and make a kissing noise. It cracked me up," said Davis.

Detmer often showed up at fall scrimmages with a sack of candy. After the session, he would hand out treats to his offensive line and other players.

"There's Ty again," laughed one player. "He's politicking so they'll vote him captain again." Ty Detmer became the first three-year team captain in BYU school history. Teammates loved him, coaches counted on him. He had the ability to lift those around him to a new level, taking up slack and performing at greater heights play after play. He led by example and used everything at his disposal to inspire greater execution for wins, including words and sometimes a little tug or push.

His touchdown celebrations at BYU, where he'd tackle a receiver, bowl over a running back, or slap a teammate silly, are legendary. It is hard to imagine anyone enjoying the moment of victory more than the kid from San Antonio.

But in the locker room, win or lose, Detmer had the ability to put a game in perspective. After heart-breaking losses, he'd calmly tackle an army of reporters, answering questions about everything from specific plays, game preparation, strategy, play calling, injuries, and even queries about the defense. He always faced these sessions with the demeanor of a veteran full-time coach, delivering informative and precise quotes for notebooks and cameras. From his first postgame interview at Wyoming his freshman year when he threw four interceptions in a loss, to the final game of his career, a 13-13 tie with Iowa in the Holiday Bowl, Ty

Detmer had total control of his locker room demeanor. He knew when the game began and ended, and though he'd be torn up inside at times, it never showed. He'd mastered that too.

Mike Burrows, a sports writer for the Colorado Springs *Gazette Telegraph* and a longtime follower of college football, saw Detmer's first college game at Wyoming. It was a nightmare game for the future Heisman Trophy winner, a game Burrows says he won't ever forget (first game, 1988 season). He also won't forget Detmer's postgame Q & A with reporters, outside the BYU locker room. Said Burrows:

"The lingering memory I have of Ty is that night in Laramie. Not so much the way he played, in a game televised by ESPN, but the way Ty handled himself afterward. I was stunned. He was the most mature college freshman I'd ever encountered. He took every question. He could have said, 'Not tonight, fellas,' and I think we'd have understood. He explained every sack, every interception. He must have talked for 20 minutes. He said he thought he could get better. He wasn't joking. I left the press box that night thinking BYU had a great spokesman, a great ambassador, for its football program, in addition to what everybody thought was a future great player. I mean, he even thanked us for coming to the game."

When asked about an interception or a mistake, a frequent Detmer response would be: "Well, sir, I guess I threw a bad pass and the other guy caught it." The simplicity with which he dissected a game postmortem became an art; many times his answers were so indisputably clear, they were actually funny.

The first mistake everybody made with Ty Detmer was judging him by his lanky frame and quiet persona. The man is nothing like the package.

When in junior high, Ty played on an area team in a 32-team San Antonio basketball tournament which included athletes from all over the state. After three days of competition, when the all-tournament team was announced, Detmer's name was on the list.

In his senior year Ty and his teammates played Uvalde High in basketball. Uvalde's team was comprised of football players, a couple in the 240-pound range. The Uvalde student body teased Detmer by chanting "BYU-who? BYU-who? BYU-who?" since he'd committed to the Cougars the previous summer. Southwest's student body responded by chanting "Uvalde J.C.s! Uvalde J.C.s!," making fun of the opponents as only worthy of junior college athletes. Ty tore Uvalde apart. At halftime the Uvalde coach protested to officials that Ty was playing too rough, that they'd allowed him to be too aggressive on the boards and when he went after steals.

Sonny Detmer quipped to Neil Reed that evening, "Too rough? And he's too small to play major college football?"

In 1990, before the NFL draft, New York Giants general manager George Young told reporters that picking a quarterback is a very risky business because there is no science to drafting quarterbacks. Young said you shouldn't rate quarterbacks by height, weight and arm strength. "Judge them by their heart, guts and week-in/week-out performance," he said.

"He's got to have courage. The guy has to be competitive as hell. Some guys are producers. That's what we all failed to see with [Joe] Montana. We spent too much time worrying about his measureables. Everything he's doing in the NFL now is exactly what he did at Notre Dame. He finds a way to win."

Sonny Detmer, who knows his son better than any scout or coach could, is puzzled over the big mystery over Ty's size. "People think a quarterback needs to be tall. Why everybody's idea of a quarterback is a 6-5, 6-6 guy, I don't know. Those guys are generally unsuccessful. To say Ty can't play pro ball at this size and Joe Montana can—and they're the same size—doesn't make any sense. What about the size of their talent?"

Former San Francisco '49er coach Bill Walsh is generally considered a builder of quarterbacks, an expert on signal callers. Walsh claims there are more drafting mistakes made in picking quarterbacks than in picking any other position in football.

Walsh says too many NFL teams put too much faith in the strength of a quarterback's arm.

In his book *Building a Champion*, Walsh's key ingredients for a quarterback include the following:

natural competitive instincts, quick delivery, agility and movement, functional instinctive mental process (or the ability to think on one's feet, which is more than intelligence), credibility with teammates as to his ability to perform, self-confidence, resourcefulness and leadership.

Offensive guru Walsh maintains that a quarterback must lift his teammates to a higher level of performance, that it's all done by performance—not by halftime talks. It's not the dialogue in the huddle. It's the spontaneous moves, the ability to make the critical play that wins the game. [Joe] Montana can do that, Steve Young can do that. What players most look for is a quarterback with poise, a calming effect, so they know they can converse with him in the most frenzied moments, rather than a quarterback who is constantly screaming at them. Leadership in a quarterback does not mean overt posturing. It's communicating under the most difficult circumstances.

Walsh, Ty's coaches will testify, is describing Ty Detmer. "What you see in Ty Detmer," explains BYU head coach LaVell Edwards, "is a very quiet, self-effacing, humble young man. But put him on the field and he becomes almost a raging tiger. He's very competitive, almost combative at times—a guy you really love to coach."

Continues Edwards, "Two or three years down the road he will be playing for somebody, and they'll be patting themselves on the back and saying they saw he had it all along."

The lure of the Ty Detmer story is the simple plot of a seemingly ordinary boy taking a game and playing it better than anyone before him has done. But in the process Detmer never changed, never forgot he was not bigger than the game or the forces that put him there.

Ty Detmer could be anyone's neighbor, the guy next door, the big or little brother in any American family.

On January 21, 1992, Michigan's 1991 Heisman Trophy winner Desmond Howard called a press conference in Ann Arbor. There he told the nation's press he would give up his senior year at Michigan to pursue a career in the NFL.

There is nothing wrong with a talented athlete choosing the lucrative financial rewards of professional sports over college. Of the four past Heisman winners, three (Barry Sanders [Oklahoma State], Andre Ware [Houston] and Desmond Howard) abandoned their senior year of college eligibility for the NFL. The lone holdout was Ty Detmer.

Howard told the nation that day he had nothing left to prove by returning to the college game.

He said, "There was nothing new that I could have done—maybe break a few more records, but as far as awards and accolades are concerned, once you've won the Heisman, then most people in college football think that you've done it all. All I would have been striving for if I would have come back would be helping Michigan win the national championship."

In other words, Howard got all he personally wanted.

His words formed a stark contrast to those of the 1990 winner. "My family's real down to earth," Detmer told reporters after he'd been awarded his Heisman. "Sure it would be exciting to hear the offers and things like that. But I guess growing up in Texas, you learn to stick to your word a little bit more. They've made plans for me at BYU and I've made plans for them."

Detmer ended his college career a year later in San Diego's Jack Murphy Stadium December 30, 1991. He led BYU in the Holiday Bowl to a 13-13 tie with No. 7-ranked Iowa from the Big 10 conference.

Ty Detmer broke 59 NCAA records, completing 958 of 1,530 passes for 15,031 yards and 121 touchdowns. His career passing efficiency rating of 162.7 is the best in football history. Contrary to what critics say about BYU game schedules, Ty's passes came against football powers like Penn State, Miami, UCLA, Florida State, Iowa, Texas A&M and Colorado. Note that three of these teams, Miami's Hurricanes, Florida's Seminoles, and the Buffs from Boulder, were ranked No. 1 in the nation (either before or after Ty played them). "Ty Detmer set a standard on and off the field which will never be equaled," claimed Claude Bassett, an assistant coach who recruited him from San Antonio's Southwest High.

The experts agree:

• Paul Roach, Wyoming athletic director and former
coordinator with the Oakland Raiders:
"Ty Detmer is the greatest impact player I've
ever seen."

• Florida State head coach Bobby Bowden:
"I really like his coolness. If it was baseball and
he was a pitcher, he'd be a pitcher who had every
pitch. The fast ball is there. The curveball is
there. The slider is there. We had him stopped
cold and he still was able to throw the ball across
his body to complete the pass. He found guys who
shouldn't have been open down the field."

• John Hall, *Orange County Register:*
"Ty Detmer doesn't have to apologize to anyone
for 1990. His records are legit and so is his
talent."

• UCLA coach Terry Donahue:
"He was sensational. The guy is like Houdini.
He's better than we thought he was. He's a
tremendous athlete."

• Mike Waldner, of the *Daily Breeze* in San Diego:
"Detmer can move a team in the air with the
best of them. He's poised, clever and quick. He

looks defensive backs off his target like a 10-year NFL veteran. Detmer has great touch. He knows where his receivers will be on the field. He delivers the ball to them as they break open. When his receivers are covered, he scrambles and picks up yards on his own. Sometimes he'll run, stop and find an open man with an accurate pass. You can go on and on. The guy is an outstanding college quarterback."

• Penn State coach Joe Paterno:

"He is an amazing kid—he doesn't say boo out there. You like to play against kids like that even if you would lose. I thought Ty was the best quarterback we've probably ever played against in all of my years at Penn State. He has a great feel for things. You rush five men and he knows you're in some kind of man-to-man. Then he'll come off the drop and get it to his backs going one-on-one. You rush three, he can sense that you're rushing three. He just sits in there and waits until something develops downfield. If you get to an all-out blitz he reads the blitz real well. He's a superior competitor."

• Earle Bruce, the former Ohio State coach who is now at Colorado State:

"Ty Detmer is the best I've ever seen. When I was at Ohio State, we had the best quarterbacks in the country probably right in that league, and we faced all of them, including the guy that's down at Denver [John Elway]. I want to tell you something, the guy [Ty Detmer] can throw the football. He is amazing. He is the best quarterback in college football. I have seen all the quarterbacks that you can possibly imagine playing pro football, but I want to tell you I've watched this guy for three years and I've watched him tonight and all season. He throws the ball better than anybody I've ever seen."

• Wyoming head coach Joe Tiller:
"Detmer is an outstanding player. Maybe there is nobody that good who has ever played on the collegiate level. He is a great, great competitor, and obviously a talented player."

• San Diego State coach Al Luginbill:
"You can't take a single play off against this young man, or you pay."

• LaVell Edwards, head BYU football coach, after Ty's junior year:
"Inside that little frame burns a furnace. Ty has shadowed the NCAA record book; he has been consistent week in and week out in a roller coaster season when he's been in and out as the frontrunner [for the Heisman Trophy] and

30

handled the pressure as well as anyone. His passing efficiency is...the best of all time."

FOUR

HUMBLING THE EXPERTS

Despite all the experts who have recognized Ty's unique gifts, a lot of other experts predicted Ty Detmer would never make it as a Texas high school quarterback. Others scoffed at the idea he could be a major college quarterback. Still others laugh at the idea of Ty Detmer in the NFL. It is all part of our culture: America is hung up on experts.

Experts tell us what to eat, how to sleep, what our dreams mean, who our next president will be, what the hidden messages are behind the headlines. Experts predict who should and shouldn't win the Super Bowl. America loves experts. *Webster's Dictionary* defines an expert as "one who is very skillful or highly trained and informed in some special field."

We subscribe to magazines and newsletters so experts can tell us how to invest our money and what cars and vacuums to buy. There are people who stay awake to watch the nightly round of experts expertly decipher all the events of the day. Only then can these watchers and listeners sleep easily in their very informed state of expertly-settled rest.

Unless college football establishes a national playoff to ensure an annual champion, a panel of coaches and writers will continue to vote on the *USA Today*-CNN and Associated Press wire polls, securely crowning football teams as the best in the land. They are the experts. At halftime and before kickoffs, America's football fans listen to talking heads of highly paid experts tell us what we are about to see (or what we've just seen). It's called expert commentary, perspective.

For most of his young life, Ty Detmer of Southwest High and Brigham Young University faced a diet of expert opinion on how and when he would succeed or fail as an athlete.

Experts said he appeared too fragile to play major college football, yet he won a Heisman Trophy, symbolizing the best college player in the land. They said he was too weak to take hits. But he missed finishing just one football game in high school or college due to injury—the Texas A&M Holiday Bowl his junior year. They said he appeared too small, although he's taller than Fran Tarkenton and casts about the same silhouette as Joe Montana. They said Detmer had a weak arm which made him basically useless on a football field; yet others with stronger arms in college and the NFL continue to miss open receivers with annoying regularity.

Max Emfinger, a graduate of Baylor University of the Southwest Conference, publishes a talent and recruiting service. This service ranks high school talent around the country, specifically in the state of Texas. Emfinger is an expert. The great populous states of Florida, Texas and California are considered the hotbed of high school football. These are the watering holes college coaches go to, seeking future stars. In a numbers game, chances are, if you want a premium player, Texas, Florida or California will grow you one.

When young Detmer concluded his junior year of high school by breaking a bevy of Texas single-season passing records, Emfinger, a consultant for All-America services, ranked the star from San Antonio's Southwest High as the best quarterback in Texas. Emfinger put him on his gold list as the best prep quarterback in the land.

It didn't take a rocket scientist to put Ty on that list. Just months earlier, the Amarillo Chamber of Commerce named Detmer the 1985 Texas Football Player of the Year. On Amarillo's panel of experts were hall-of-fame football players Tommy Nobis, Bob Lilly, Bobby Lane, Sammy Baugh and Doak Walker. All living legends.

That summer, just before his senior year, Ty Detmer verbally committed to play college football at BYU. He made that decision early and then witnessed an entire state practically turn its back on him.

To the expert Emfinger, how good could Ty Detmer be if he was going to school outside the Southwest Conference, outside the state of Texas?

That summer, after Detmer's announcement to go to BYU, Emfinger requested some tapes of Ty's junior year so he could make an "informed" list for an upcoming All-America team. A Detmer family friend, Neil Reed, took tapes to Emfinger, who promptly cut to pieces the young quarterback's performance. Legends Doak Walker, Tommy Nobis and Sammy Baugh loved Detmer. But suddenly Emfinger knew more than all of them and it was very apparent he wasn't going to recommend that the young San Antonio quarterback be an All-American.

In Emfinger's Houston driveway, Reed took the tapes out of the recruiting guru's hands and told him he'd blown it. Then he promptly sent copies of the tapes to broadcasters and sportswriters all over the USA. When Bally's announced its 1986 All-American team, Ty Detmer made the list.

That was young Ty's first taste of expert analysis.

A second-team all-state player as a Southwest High junior in 1985, Ty, after committing to BYU in his senior year in 1986, didn't make the coaches' first-team all-state roster. Nor was he named the best quarterback in the city of San Antonio. He and his Dragons didn't have as much success that season, but his having signed with BYU may have been what disqualified him in the eyes of some Texans. (In 1985 the San Antonio City

Player of the Year, as tabbed by the city newspaper, was running back Jerry Arseno of Holmes High.)

Emfinger has said both privately and publicly that he could guarantee that Clark High School quarterback Mike Maschek would be a better college quarterback than Ty Detmer of Southwest. Maschek later accepted a scholarship to play at Purdue, where he was on the team between 1987 and 1988. He then transferred to Trinity Junior College, ending up eventually at University of Virginia at Richmond, where he played in only seven games.

Three years later, in 1989, Ty Detmer, finishing his sophomore year at BYU, earned his first All-America citation, posting a 175.5 pass efficiency rating. That rating ranked Detmer second behind Jim McMahon as the most accurate single-season passer in college football history. Two seasons later, Ty ended his undergraduate days as the most efficient career passer of all time, throwing for nearly eight miles. Detmer is the first college football player to pass for 15,000 yards (or 14,000, or 13,000, or for that matter, 12,000 yards) in college football history.

Ty Detmer ended a sterling college career as college football's all-time passing yardage leader, eclipsing 59 NCAA records. In four years in Provo, Detmer passed for 15,031 yards and 121 touchdowns. His career pass efficiency rating of 162.7 established a major college standard.

But records and marks are just like all the other handles experts use to generate their informed opinions. Although many of Detmer's statistical triumphs came against football powerhouses like Penn State, Florida State, and Miami and speak volumes in and of themselves, the best argument in behalf of Ty Detmer is that he simply makes plays and gets the job done.

Sonny Detmer scoffs at the criticism of his son's size and arm strength, asking, "Where did those scouts play football?"

Ty bristles at any mention he's a midget, or the same size as 5-8 Doug Flutie of Boston College, who left the NFL for the Canadian Football League.

Ty Detmer is 6 foot 1/2 inch tall. His arm length is greater than normal, stretching 38 inches, which other experts say makes his throwing motion more like that of a 6-3 player. Playing behind 6-6 and 6-8 offensive linemen at BYU, Detmer never had a problem seeing receivers downfield.

Imagine, the man who rewrote the book on college passing not making it in the NFL. The *San Diego Union*, longstanding witness to Ty's acumen, called that notion "mind-boggling."

The week of Detmer's final collegiate game in Jack Murphy Stadium (against No. 7-ranked Iowa, December 30, 1991,) the *Union* ran a few comments by NFL scouts. The most vocal critic of Detmer his last two record-breaking seasons was Mel Kiper, Jr., who received the most attention because of his affiliation as an expert analyst for ESPN.

Here is Mel Kiper, Jr. on Detmer: "He's a late-rounder, free-agent type prospect, a guy who might be able to hang on as a backup quarterback with some teams. He's a great college quarterback with very marginal pro potential."

NFL scout Joel Buchsbaum seems to agree: "A highly efficient player who gets the most out of his ability but who may not have enough size, physical strength or arm strength to play in the NFL. If he does make it, it will probably be in a Gary Kubiak-type backup role." [Kubiak was the Denver Bronco backup to John Elway before retiring to coach at Texas A&M.]

As Kiper explained in a *San Diego Union* article of December 28, 1991: "This is to take nothing away from the kid. I don't like answering questions about him because it makes you seem very critical of a guy who shouldn't be criticized for what he's doing now.

"He deserves everything he's gotten. He's probably one of the best college quarterbacks I've ever seen, and not just because of his numbers. He has that Doug Flutie ability of a magical quarterback.... But when you look at pro prospects, it's a totally different ball game.

"He has all the things you need except for size and arm strength, and those are two things you need most in the NFL. Arm strength and size are two things you can't help. You either are 6-2 or you aren't. In his case, he's not only short, he's fragile, frail."

Kiper predicted, on record, that Detmer could be the 15th quarterback taken in the 1992 NFL draft.

Thrown the question over and over, BYU head coach LaVell Edwards keeps his answer very simple: "Ty Detmer can play in the NFL. He'll stick with some team and when the starting quarterback goes down, he'll come in and be very successful. He might even surprise people by not giving the starting job back."

Chris Wojcieschowski, *Los Angeles Times* columnist, provided an interesting comment on Kiper's expertise: "And a memo to NFL draft guru Mel Kiper, who boldly guarantees that Detmer will hardly make a ripple in the pros: Weren't you the same guy who ranked Houston's Andre Ware, Utah's Scott Mitchell, Idaho's John Friez, Washington's Cary Conklin, Maine's Mike Buck and Louisiana State's Tommy Hodson above eventual 1990 No. 1 draft choice Jeff George of Illinois?"

Dick Vermeil, ABC-TV analyst and former Philadelphia Eagle head coach, predicted Detmer would have limitations because of his size. "But you can't do any more than throw completed passes and that's what he does. He's extremely accurate. He throws the difficult ball very well. He sees the field. Where he's going to be in regard to the NFL, I don't know. But I do know this: He throws completions."

Some experts predicted the nation saw the last of Ty Detmer at his final college game on December 30, 1991, the night he completed 29 of 44 passes for 350 yards and two touchdowns on No. 7-ranked Iowa. It was only Iowa.

40

Then there was the voice of another expert, ESPN color analyst Gary Danielson, in San Diego that night: "Ty will be disappointed when he gets to the NFL because their offenses aren't as sophisticated as BYU."

Mike Holmgren, former offensive coordinator for the San Francisco '49ers, former quarterback coach at BYU, and current head coach for the Green Bay Packers, predicts Detmer will have a long and fruitful career in professional football. "He will make some team very happy. I don't like to make predictions on what round he will go in. But there is no question in my mind he will have a fine career in the NFL."

Here are a few facts which ought to be considered when pondering the professional fate of Ty Detmer:

Including the injury to Denver's John Elway in the 1991 NFL playoffs, 10 NFL quarterbacks in that season alone suffered injuries, which played a big role in the outcome of divisional races. These quarterbacks included big starters like Randall Cunningham of Philadelphia and Steve Young of San Francisco.

It didn't matter how big these quarterbacks were. It didn't matter how fast, how strong or how far they could throw the football. They went down. The NFL is now in need of quarterbacks. The position is the highest paid in the league for a good reason. A team cannot have enough good quarterbacks on its roster.

The size of NFL quarterbacks has little relationship to professional success. Name a 6-5 quarterback who

41

has led his team to a Super Bowl in the past 10 years. You have to think hard. Height is overrated.

Joe Montana and Johnny Unitas are generally considered among the best that ever played. They are not significantly bigger in stature than Ty Detmer.

Jim McMahon, who is injury prone, is the exact same height as Ty Detmer and has lasted in the NFL for 10 years and owns a Super Bowl ring. His contribution at Philadelphia in 1991 earned him a photo on the cover of *Sports Illustrated.*

If the NFL isn't smart enough to draft Ty, the CFL isn't a bad place to play. A wider field might even play into Detmer's hands. Warren Moon went to Canada after his Washington career and now is considered one of the NFL's best quarterbacks (with Houston). Joe Theisman came to the Washington Redskins from the CFL after being picked 99th.

What do NFL scouts know? Johnny Unitas was pulled off a bulldozer in Pittsburgh after coach Paul Brown saw what he could do in a camp. Pittsburgh's Dan Marino was taken after Todd Blackledge, who never made it. Joe Montana was drafted 82nd after winning a national championship and two Cotton Bowls for Notre Dame. These NFL scouts are the same people who advised that Jerry Tagge (Nebraska) and Scott Hunter (Alabama) were NFL caliber quarterbacks because they were 6-3 and had great arms. These experts compared Tage and Hunter to Chicago Bear Bobby Douglas: they could throw a football through a brick wall. But the receivers couldn't hang on to these "no-touch fireballs" so the power was wasted. Tage and Hunter never made it in the NFL.

The NFL? Experts? Opinions? "I don't care what they say; you never know until you play," says Ty. "There was a question if I could make it in college; I didn't know until I tried. With the NFL, all I know is nobody knows until I have the chance. I know I'll get out there and compete with anyone. I think I've proven I can be a leader. I want to play in the NFL just because they say I can't. Oh, and I'd like to play NFL football so I can make some money to go hunting."

FIVE

PAW PAW AND
MAW MAW DETMER

On Friday, October 10, 1986, the Dragons of San Antonio's Southwest High defeated the Minutemen of Memorial High 47-0, riding on the arm of their All-America quarterback Ty Detmer.

That night in Southwest's stadium, Detmer sliced apart the Minutemen as if they were cardboard cutouts. He was their worst nightmare. Detmer shattered four city records, completing 27 of 44 passes for 435 yards and seven touchdowns. Those numbers signified somebody dominating at that level. On the next level, major college play, those numbers would become routine.

In the stadium that night sat Hubert and Doris Detmer, affectionately referred to in the Detmer clan as Paw Paw and Maw Maw. These two grandparents were Ty's No. 1 fans.

Ty's seven touchdown passes that night set a new city mark for high school career touchdown passes. It gave him 58, surpassing the old record of 54 thrown by

Tommy Kramer at Lee from 1971-72. Kramer went on to play at Rice University. He then played for the Minnesota Vikings in the NFL.

That night Detmer also broke the city record for touchdown passes in a single game, bettering the five thrown by Brackenridge's Victor Castillo against Houston Spring Branch in 1962.

That night Detmer's 435 yards through the air even broke his own city record of 430, which he set during playoffs the previous season against Calallen. He also set a state record for career passing yardage with 6,245 (breaking the mark of 6,190 by Gary Kubiak at Houston St. Pius from 1975-78). Kubiak went on to a solid NFL career and ended his professional days by replacing John Elway in the 1991 NFL playoffs. Ty went on to increase his own mark to a high school career total of 8,005 passing yards.

Before the 1986 season started, Sonny Detmer told Minuteman coach E.C. Lee that if Ty had a chance to get those marks against Lee's team, he'd let him rip. Lee replied: "I hope I'm there when he gets it."

Paw Paw and Maw Maw wouldn't have missed it for the world.

Paw Paw Detmer, the patriarch of the family, is described as the calming force in the family. His wife, Maw Maw, served as the shaker and mover, disciplinarian, and detail person. Paw Paw retired from a career at the Monsanto Corporation. Maw Maw served as vice president of several banks in Indiana and Texas.

Maw Maw and Paw Paw Detmer were known as the Salt of the Earth.

Having the right genes on your side is a big plus. Ty Detmer's lineage is exactly that. On his mother's side, his ancestors were among the first settlers of the vast Lone Star state, an adventuresome landscape dotted with longhorn cattle, Mexicans and frontiersmen.

Hubert Detmer immersed himself in the fire of Indiana basketball, leading his Rising Sun Shiners to their first sectional championship in 1930. Excluding Hubert Detmer's sectional title, the Shiners drew a blank from 1911 to 1984—73 years.

Paw Paw Detmer, straight from the movie *Hoosiers*, taught his grandson that if you played a game, you played to have fun, but you also played to win. Nobody plays to lose.

Paw Paw tossed baseballs and footballs to Ty when he was a toddler. He witnessed Ty's record-breaking performances at Southwest High and tuned in to BYU games via satellite. Paw Paw and Maw Maw Detmer supported their grandson by living his triumphs and wiping away his tears. Ravaged by cancer, Paw Paw survived long enough to see a Heisman Trophy placed on his living room fireplace mantel. Three months later he died. Ty Detmer's Heisman and all of his major trophies and awards may still be seen in the sun parlor of Maw Maw Detmer's San Antonio home.

Paw Paw Detmer was born in the farming town of Rising Sun, a small rural community near the border of

Indiana and Ohio. Friends remember him as a loving, kind man, the kind of friend you never forget because he will never forget you.

Paw Paw's first job was testing cream on its way to the train station en route to processing.

He served in the Army, a member of the 44th Battalion based in Biloxi, Mississippi, and fought in the Pacific Theatre when World War II broke out. He met his wife, Doris Buchholz, a girl from Beaumont, Texas, while in Biloxi.

Sonny was their only child.

Forever, Sonny will credit his father for inspiring Ty's love of football, his *furor for winning*, his commitment to the game, and his fundamental sportsmanship. "I had to be the parent," Doris says. "I did the discipline. He did the playing. He was Sonny's best friend."

When Sonny, Betty and one-year-old Ty moved to San Antonio, Paw Paw and Maw Maw picked up their belongings in Cincinnati and moved there too, settling on the same street. Doris worked as the vice president of a bank in Alamo Heights and Hubert took an early retirement for health reasons. Home all day, Paw Paw Detmer's highlight of the day was when his grandchildren came home from school so he could play with them.

"He was kind of a baby-sitter when we were growing up," says Ty. "He would hit fly balls, play catch with us. Shoot baskets. Go in the back yard with us. He was never too busy to do it. He would always hit us ground balls and pop flies in the yard. He would see if we could back-hand them. This is when we were six and seven years old. He always made it a challenge for us."

Hubert Detmer always competed and played with the kids and rigged it so they'd win. That always puzzled Sonny. Paw Paw wanted the kids to feel the excitement and thrill of winning.

"I would play cards with him, and I would get so mad at him because he would let me win all the time," says Sonny. "But the thing is, you got used to winning. He did the same thing with the kids. I was just the opposite. I'd beat Ty and Koy every time I could. That probably balanced things out, because he played with them a lot more than I did. The thing is, I'm not sure my way is the way to do it. They won, they won, they won. They're used to winning. Koy turned 16 and beat me at golf. I've never beaten him since."

"We miss Paw Paw so much but know he rests in peace," says Maw Maw. "Our many precious memories will keep him alive in our hearts forever. He was such an inspiration to all of us. His courage, love and wonderful faith never left him."

Hubert Detmer battled prostate cancer for five years. During that time he suffered great pain and discomfort as that bane of mankind, that cheater of life which no money and no power has conquered, ran its course.

In 1990, the Heisman year, Ty kept in constant contact with his grandfather and would report to his Utah friends, "He's not doing well. Not at all."

During the most pressure-packed months of his life, Ty never forgot his grandfather and in a sense played with a fury as if every play, every pass, and touchdown would keep Paw Paw alive longer, making him hang on to see the kickoff the next weekend.

Doris said watching Ty play on television became more meaningful for her husband during that 1990 season.

"It was so important to Hubert. It gave him something to be here for. It kept him going."

Paw Paw hung on that year, carefully watching the Heisman race and Ty's antics on and off the field. On December 5, the Detmer family gathered around a television set and watched the Heisman Trophy ceremonies on national television. They had to do it in Kingsville, Texas, where Sonny's Mission High team prepared to play Madison in a 5A playoff game. While his family sat poised in a room under Javelina Stadium, Ty stood in the patio area of a hotel in Honolulu (where the Cougars were to play the University of Hawaii later that evening), a network satellite linkup capturing him with coaches and players, awaiting the announcement. They'd been there for more than an hour, the hot portable studio lights literally roasting them in the humid Hawaiian midday sun.

The moment abruptly arrived: the CBS commentator's voice on the television spoke the magic words, the loudest Paw Paw ever heard in his life.

"Join me in letting the country know the name of the winner of the 1990 Heisman Award. His name is Ty Detmer of Brigham Young."

The room in Kingsville erupted in applause. Sonny and Betty quietly embraced, tears welling up in their eyes.

Koy broke the moment by handing Sonny a handkerchief.

"What's that for?" asked Sonny. "Um, boy, this is a rough one."

Ty's sister Dee fought back her tears, feeling exhilaration and a sense of relief. Her big brother had done it. All the polls, all the criticism, all the hype. It was over. Dee had helped Ty develop his scrambling ability during their growing up years when she used to chase him around the house with a golf club. "Your heart stops," Dee said. "It seemed like forever. We had been hoping for this. Hoping and hoping."

Sonny's Mission Eagles defeated San Antonio Madison 59-17 that night. Koy threw for more than 390 yards. BYU lost to Hawaii 59-28. Paw Paw Detmer died March 12, 1991. His death came 81 days after those Heisman ceremonies.

The night of his grandfather's death, the Professional Athletes Assisting Youth sports organization named Ty Detmer the San Antonio male

51

amateur athlete of the year at its annual banquet. Sonny received the award on behalf of his son.

"I know Sonny was hurting, but I told him to go accept it for Ty," said Doris. "I told him I knew it would be hard on him, but Hubert would have wanted him to go."

A Detmer legacy began and ended that day: life in the family without Paw Paw.

SIX

SONNY DETMER

On September 15, 1990 Washington State led BYU 28-7 through three quarters in Cougar Stadium at Provo and a crowd of 68,848 fell silent.

In the next 15 minutes Ty Detmer led BYU to a remarkable 36-point scoring run that buried the Cougars from Pullman. Detmer threw for four second-half touchdowns as the Cougars scored 43 second-half points (36 in a school-record fourth quarter). The Cougars won the game 50-36.

It was a remarkable comeback. Detmer completed 32 of 50 passes (64 percent) for 448 yards and five touchdowns. His quest for the first Heisman Trophy ever awarded to a player from the Rockies was alive and well.

The previous year Washington State had hung on to whip BYU 46-41. Coach Mike Price chirped that BYU coach LaVell Edwards got the last laugh when a seagull flew overhead and bombed Mike outside the locker room before he got to the team bus.

Now it was Detmer, not a seagull, who bombed Price and his Cougars. But to Price, it probably felt warmly the same.

Detmer repeated performances like the one that Saturday several times in his career. A quarterback like Ty doesn't grow on trees, or dive from them either.

If you want to find the key to Ty Detmer, go talk to his father, Sonny Detmer, the offensive wizard and lover of games. Sonny Detmer never met a game he didn't love to play. And when it came to sports, there were few he didn't master. He was a competitor with a knack for hustle and a penchant for winning. As a baseball centerfielder his range included everything behind second base to the fence. He caught fly balls as if packing a Willie Mays basket. At the plate Sonny pounded power line drives through the alleys like laser-guided missiles.

On the basketball court, Sonny owned loose balls; he was a go-to guy. But on the football field, between the yardline stripes, Sonny really excelled. His soft hands as a receiver drew passes like a magnet. He developed a genius for picking the seams, the open blind spots in a defense. If the ball traveled to the general vicinity, Sonny would deliver a big play.

The vacant lot across from his house in Lawrenceburg, Indiana became a Field of Dreams. There in that sandlot arena a small army of neighborhood kids gathered to play their guts out, lighting their hearts on fire with the thrill of making play after play. In the Detmer backyard hung a hoop, like most households in Indiana, the Hoosier State that hatched Larry Bird, groomed the great John Wooden, and survived Bobby Knight. The grass underneath that basketball hoop got worn down to naked ground from the pounding of basketballs, victim of at least a million dribbles. The staccato sound of a bouncing ball and the cadence of a quarterback's count were music to Sonny Detmer's ears. The rush of adrenalin from banging out a big play became an opiate, an addiction Sonny could never get over. And God gave him the talent to impart it to others (particularly his two sons).

People get into coaching for a lot of reasons. Sometimes it's the starved, yearning cry of a hungry ego. Or it is the second-life incarnate of an over-the-hill jock. But sometimes it's the love of the game and the heartfelt duty to teach the skills that come with perfecting the art of play. A good coach dives into the competition and directs his players how to master it. A great coach builds players who can master the competition by themselves. It is a tune that becomes obsessive. With Sonny Detmer it did, and his obsession with games became his calling, his life.

A Texas Tech football coach once visited a high school pressbox where Sonny Detmer, the head football coach, barked down signals to coaches and quarterbacks on the field via phone lines. The coach was awestruck by the genius behind the voice ordering formations, calling plays and sizing up the opposing defense. Not since the days of Sammy Baugh's aerial circus had storied Texas football seen firepower of the forward pass like that produced by Southwest High in San Antonio and Mission High in Mission (coincidentally, the hometown of Tom Landry).

A *Sporting News* All-America wide receiver at Wharton College (Texas), Sonny Detmer went on to play baseball and basketball at Florida State. Of all the influences on Ty Detmer, none wielded more impact in this All-American's life than did his father Sonny.

Hubert and Doris Detmer had only one child. God gave them a son. They had just one chance to see he turned out OK.

Lawrenceburg, was a hotbed of competitive athletics, especially basketball, where the Hoosier State had the country's first and most famous Final Four. The NCAA fashioned its own Final Four after the state of Indiana. This was a state championship tournament where every school in Indiana, no matter how big or small, could play for the title if they kept winning until the end.

The Detmers lived in an affluent upper middle-class neighborhood where boys like Sonny were driven by nature to succeed, look at the positive side of life, and compete with each other in the classroom and on the playing field.

Friends describe Sonny Detmer as an intensely competitive and gifted athlete, who loves every minute of his life and gets the most out of hunting, fishing and playing athletics. He's a natural.

"Sonny was a great, great athlete and a super guy," remembers former team mate Dr. Ron Bateman of Fort Collins, Colorado. "He had the best pair of hands I've ever seen. He played centerfield in baseball and end in football. If the ball got anywhere past second base, it was his. He'd dive and slide for everything that came his way in baseball. He was a tremendous hitter at the plate. He was quite amazing. In football it was not a surprise he was named an All-American receiver in junior college. He made me an all-conference quarterback because he caught everything I threw at him. He wasn't big, just 6 foot and 155 pounds dripping wet, but he could get open and make the play. He was a go-to guy."

The Lawrenceburg Tigers had a tremendous basketball team, led by 6-9 Jim Caldwell, who later played for Georgia Tech and went on to a career in the NBA. "Sonny starred in all the sports. He was an incredible baseball player, but that is splitting hairs," said Bateman. "He was an outstanding athlete."

The Tiger basketball team consisted of Sonny, Jim, Ron and three other players (Mike Fehling, Ronnie Kinnett and Jeff Allen) who were also Sonny's boyhood friends. Of the 10 players on the Tiger basketball team, seven earned doctorates. In their senior season of 1961 (where Sonny was the youngest, at age 16, of his graduating class), this teenaged team went 20-2.

Ron lived two doors down from the Detmers and always headed there to watch Sunday's Walt Disney specials.

A vacant lot across the street served as the neighborhood athletic field. The boys played football by the professional rules: you weren't down until you were down.

In Sonny's junior year the Tigers ranked third in the state of Indiana in basketball—third among 712 schools. The team had a 21-0 record and played Madison in the first game of the sectional playoffs, losing by three points. In Indiana, in those days, there were no divisions. If you lost, you were out.

Ron's father, George E. "Bud" Bateman, one of the most respected coaches in Indiana, coached the Tigers. Bud Bateman remembers Sonny Detmer as an athlete, a super baseball player who batted left-handed and seldom struck out.

Two decades later, Bateman watched Ty Detmer on ESPN one night and without even seeing numbers or names, picked him out on the field. "My God, there is Sonny," he said.

The summer of 1990, Bud Bateman and his wife boarded up their house and took off across the country visiting friends and relatives for their 50th wedding anniversary. They went all over, stopping and staying with 22 families. "Every place I went", Bud says, "I told people I knew who'd win the Heisman Trophy that year—Ty Detmer."

Sonny met his wife Betty Spellman while at Wharton Junior College. Betty is the daughter of chiropractor Clyde Spellman and his wife Alva of El Campo, Texas (near Houston). Clyde was nicknamed "Runt" Spellman by his friends because he wasn't very big. But he didn't need to be big to make an impression on them as a fierce competitor in everything he did. Clyde died in January 1983. He never saw his grandson Ty play high school or college football.

Before his marriage, Sonny was the star football player at Wharton College in Wharton, Texas. He came to the junior college after graduating from high school in Indiana. Betty Spellman came to Wharton a year later. Her freshman year (1962-1963), Betty was crowned homecoming queen.

Sonny earned *Sporting News* All-America honors at Wharton, then transferred to Florida State, where he played baseball and basketball on scholarship. He left Tallahassee, played some semi-professional football for three years with the San Antonio Toros of the Continental Football League, then settled down to a high school coaching career. Sonny and Betty had four children, two sons and two daughters. First came Ty, then sister Dee, then Koy and last, Lori.

"Sonny had the temperament and dedication to become a good coach," says "Bud" Bateman. The first coaching job Sonny ever had was at Sommerset High in Texas, where he developed his first quarterback, Jim Bob Taylor, who later played for Southern Methodist

59

and led the Southwest Conference in passing. Taylor then transferred to Georgia Tech, where he started against Alabama and won, knocking the legendary Bear Bryant out of what would have been his final national championship.

The next coaching job Sonny landed was at Central Catholic High in San Antonio, leading the school to the Texas parochial school state championship. He then coached at Laredo-Martin, a school that had won just one game the year before. Sonny had Laredo-Martin in the playoffs his first year. At the time Ty was in the eighth grade.

From Laredo-Martin, Sonny took over the job at Southwest High in San Antonio. As head football coach, he doubled as the school's athletic director and assembled a staff which took teams regularly into the state playoffs—something which had not happened to the Dragons in any sport in 34 years.

Sonny left Southwest after Ty finished playing. That move came after a dispute with administrators and a reassignment on the staff.

BYU coach LaVell Edwards and assistant Claude Bassett helped Sonny land a job coaching at Round Valley, Arizona. The BYU connection also helped him relocate back to Texas at Mission High School a year later.

Mission High School has made the state playoffs every year since Sonny arrived in 1988, including the school's only appearance in the semifinals of the state 5A championships in the Houston Astrodome in 1990.

Sonny Detmer is an outstanding teacher of fundamental football, particularly with quarterbacks. In sons Ty and Koy, he coached two quarterbacks who combined for more than 16,000 yards in high school. Apparently, they are the only two players in high school history (siblings or not) to exceed 3,000 yards individually, in each of their junior and senior years.

As a junior at Southwest High (Class 4A), Ty passed for 3,551 yards in 13 games. As a junior at Mission (Class 5A), Koy passed for 3,685 yards in 14 games. In Ty's senior year he threw for 3,337 in 10 games. Koy's senior year stats totalled 3,681. Koy ended his high school career at Mission by throwing for 8,221 yards, breaking Huntsville High's Steve Clements' state record of 8,204. (Clements broke Ty's 1985 state record of 8,005 yards. Incidentally, Clements as of this writing has transferred to BYU from the University of Texas, joining LaVell Edwards' stable of promising quarterbacks.)

Ty's introduction to football was immediate. The first night after his birth on October 30, 1967 in San Marcos, Texas, his father held him in his arms while sitting in a rocking chair. Together, Sonny says, they watched Monday Night Football on ABC. The Kansas City Chiefs were playing.

Sonny has been a football coach since 1969 and Ty got used to being around the football field and practice sessions as soon as he could walk.

It rubbed off. Ty wants to be a coach just like his father someday.

"He's as big a part of it as anybody," says Ty. "Going to games with him. Watching his teams play. Being a ball boy. You can't beat being on the field as an elementary school kid at a high school game."

There were always coaching meetings in the Detmer home on Sunday evenings. "It was always fun to lay down on the floor watching them run the film backward and forward," says Ty. "We were exposed to a lot more of it—maybe not even knowing we were at the time."

Sonny Detmer is into hero worship and he's never shied away from taking pride in his children, particularly the accomplishments of his oldest son, Ty. The feeling is mutual.

In grade school, a boyhood friend once informed Ty of a dilemma in the boy's life—his parents were divorcing and he had to choose to live with his mother or his father. The question seemed odd to Ty. One day while riding with Betty, Ty explained the dilemma of his friend. "Well, I know who I'd go with," said Ty. "I'd go with Sonny." Those words pierced Betty Detmer's heart, but she passed it off. She knew Ty didn't mean those words to hurt her feelings. After a lifetime of living with Sonny herself, she knew what Ty meant. Sonny represented fun and games. She represented vacuuming floors and scrubbing pots and pans. "I guess scrubbing floors wasn't as appealing as what Sonny does," she says.

Whenever Sonny comes in the door, everybody in the Detmer household perks up, explains Betty.

"Sonny is a dreamer of dreams," she says. "I always told the kids I was not a dreamer; their dad was. I have always been here to help them with their dreams. I am a doer and a helper. Sonny is the one who sets dreams in the minds of the kids. When I met Sonny I latched on to his dreams. It is the same with the kids."

Sonny believes Ty belongs to San Antonio, Texas and that Utah and the rest of America got him on loan for awhile. Sonny is pleased Ty has shown what he can do.

When Sonny landed the job at Mission High, he took over from coach Rusty Dowling, who also knew how to air it out. The Eagles of Mission High produced Lupe Rodriquez, Jim Lee (Rice) and Frank Hernandez (Kansas State).

"Don't kid yourself," says BYU Texas recruiter Claude Bassett, "Sonny Detmer is the modern guru of the forward pass in Texas. Nobody else is even close."

Sonny jokes that as long as Texas high schools use baseball coaches to coach defensive secondaries, he'll throw the football with his teams. He says, "People in Texas finally are paying attention to the throwing game. In the past, you could never remember an outstanding quarterback who was a Texan. Then you had Andre Ware (at Dickinson and the University of Houston), then you had Ty. Then, you had Ty and David Klingler (Stratford and Houston), Alex Van Pelt (San Antonio and Pittsburgh), then Tommy Maddox (Hurst Bell and UCLA). All at once the best quarterbacks in the nation are coming from Texas. And in the future you've got Steve Clements, Chuck Clements, Ryan Huffman, and Koy."

Just as Ty finished his career at BYU, little brother Koy became the all-time leading passer in Texas and committed to Colorado. Koy idolized Ty. But he would not follow his brother to BYU.

Sonny remembers when Ty and Koy were growing up. He took them to play golf with a friend in San Antonio. Koy joined Sonny; Ty played with the friend in a match against the other two. After Ty and his partner won a hole, they proceeded to the next tee box near a fence separating the course from the freeway. Koy walked towards the next tee. He was pretty sore after Ty won the hole. Trailing Koy, Ty took his driver out of the bag, and while walking a few paces behind his brother, poked Koy in the butt. Koy wheeled around, dropped his bag and charged Ty. The two stood toe to toe having a donnybrook right there next to the freeway as passing motorists gawked.

Sonny stood and laughed. "It was the funniest thing I ever saw," he said.

SEVEN

SOUTHWEST HIGH SCHOOL—IT'S A JUNGLE OUT THERE

San Antonio's Southwest High School had the reputation as a loser. It stood in a blighted area in the jungle part of a city nobody mistook for the Garden of Eden. Mostly Hispanics and blacks, poor and emotionally tortured children, many raised in homes with no fathers, wandered down its halls. In a community replete with drugs, muggings and even murder, Southwest High drew its student body from one part of the city you don't find in travel brochures on the Alamo. This is the school Sonny Detmer molded into an arena for athletic champions, a sports powerhouse earning respect and turning a miracle. This is the school where Ty Detmer learned to scratch and fight for every first down left open for the taking. The Detmers ignited a fire inside a smoldering skeleton of a school. Then they left in controversy, knives protruding from their backs.

In 1983 Sonny Detmer took a job at Southwest High as athletic director and head football coach. He assembled a staff of coaches who loved to coach kids. It was like rays of sunlight breaking through to a dense jungle floor.

Southwest High had not sent an athletic team to a state playoff in 34 years. Why should anybody care about playing sports and having fun when it was a daily struggle to just wear some decent clothes, find some regular people food, and stay out of jail?

When BYU assistant football coach Claude Bassett first saw Southwest High School in 1986, with its fortified fences and yards, he said it looked more like a bomb shelter than a school.

Southwest's football program was a joke. As Ty Detmer etched out a career that would make him the most famous alumni the Dragons ever had, his father, the football coach, played the role Spencer Tracy played in the film version of another real-life miracle, *Boys Town*.

What would it be like to coach a team whose players included a car thief, a drunk and a drug pusher? (And those three were the good guys.) Well, Sonny did it.

The fact that 16-year-old Ty Detmer earned the distinction of 1985 Texas Player of the Year in his junior year at such a school was not only a major personal accomplishment, it made Sonny Detmer a candidate for the Nobel Peace Prize. If only the Swedes knew.

In Sonny's first year, the Dragons went 2-8. The next year, 1984, with sophomore Ty at the helm, they improved to 3-6-1. That same year Sonny asked his friend, Neil Reed, to join the staff. He also added E.C. Lee, a 6-6 disciplinarian whom players called "Deputy Dawg." Other additions included Kevin Schuler, Denny Schoemer, Tim Funk and Bill Lehman.

Neil Reed told Sonny to give him Tim Funk and he'd take over the receiver corps. Funk grew up in San Antonio and later played for Jim Wacker on his Division III national championship team at Texas Lutheran (1975-1977). A member of the 1984 U.S. Olympic handball team as a goalie, Funk brought a myriad of unconventional drills to Southwest. These included juggling the ball, catching three footballs in succession, and juggling balls while riding a unicycle. In skeleton passing drills with the defensive backs, Funk and other coaches created a friendly competition. The losers had to hold the drinking hose for the winners come break time.

"We tried to challenge these athletes. They were hungry to win but just didn't know how," said Funk.

"I haven't met a better offensive mind anywhere than Sonny Detmer. Neil Reed was the backbone, the rest of us were the appendages, Sonny was the genius. But Sonny needed Reed because he knew how it was in the big time. Sonny is a genius. In a game, Sonny has already thought the entire game through. He has it all in his mind. He was fun to watch. At the end of a close game, he'd stand with his left foot in front of his right;

his index finger and thumb would be used to curl his hair. I would say to the other coaches, 'Holy cow, here it comes' and footballs would start flying all over the place. He'd connect with Ty and I'd swear there were 11 receivers in an opponent's defensive secondary. They'd be crossing, curling and streaking all over the place. Nobody cranks it up like Sonny. Not anywhere."

At first, only two eighth graders and two seventh graders had showed up for football, feeding Southwest High's varsity. In no time, Lee had 12, then 62, players feeding into the junior varsity program.

Meanwhile Reed, a former assistant basketball coach to Adolph Rupp at Kentucky, helped Sonny retool the Dragon offense, moving a big 6-6 tight end out for 5-8 Dennis Ray. They needed to do something with the backs in the passing game, complementing Kevin Jennings and Mario Laque. Reed suggested they send the backs out on pass routes. Sonny wanted to keep them in for blocking. Reed insisted if the backs ran in the flat and a linebacker on defense followed, it would be just like a block. Reed won the argument with the offense-minded Sonny. Sometimes it's tough converting even the geniuses.

The Dragons discovered one back, Herman Loving, an elephant of a boy. At one point that season he caught 28 of 29 balls thrown his way.

The following year, 1985, Southwest did something for the first time in school history—the Dragons made the state playoffs, going 10-0 in the regular season. Ty broke nearly every city and Texas state passing record, completing 209 of 371 passes for 3,551 yards and 36 touchdowns. He was intercepted 10 times, but the Amarillo Chamber of Commerce didn't care when, in 1986, they added Ty's name to the legends of Texas football by crowning him 1985's best football player in Texas. That's like Zeus, Apollo, and Arius, parting the clouds on Mt. Olympus and telling Ty, "Grab your helmet and football, boy, and come pick out a toga and a throne." Only one other junior, Billy Sims, had achieved similar honors.

The Dragons' state class 4A title hopes sank, however, in the regional round playoff with Calallen in a game that would go down in Texas history as one of the worst officiated games of the decade. Southwest had nine defensive players hobbled by injuries before the game. The officials lost control of the game to the extent that one player was injured for life in a fierce tackle that was made long after the play should have been called dead. A deputy sheriff from Calallen was buying a hot dog during a timeout when Lee's daughter heard him say, "That Detmer guy sure is having a great game even if they're getting screwed."

That night Ty threw for 438 yards, but Reed claims he actually tossed for 634 yards—more than 200 yards passing got called back on questionable penalties and phantom fumbles. "It made you sick," moaned Reed.

Southwest ended the season 12-1, the best year of football the Dragons ever enjoyed. Both receivers, Kevin

Jennings and Dennis Ray, earned all-state honors. Losers got a taste of winning. Kids with the worries of adults learned to play and have fun like kids again.

In the 1986 season (Ty's senior year), during the game with Pleasanton High, Ty threw two back-to-back touchdown passes which traveled 63 and 65 yards in the air. He called all his plays that night like he had all season. Ty had 557 yards in just under three quarters. It was a Texas single-game record. That total would have been higher if Daryl Davis, a 6-3 lightning-quick halfback hadn't dropped a 40-yard Detmer pass while streaking down the sidelines for a score. Nevertheless, Southwest won.

The Dragons went 7-3 that season as BYU-bound Ty threw for 3,320 yards and 32 touchdowns on 206 of 362 passes. He ended his high school career with 8,005 yards and 71 touchdowns, both Texas passing records. That 1986 passing record ranked him as the No. 4 passer in U.S. high school history. Only Ron Cuccia (Wilson High in Los Angeles, 1975-77) with 8,804, John White (Metainie Country Day, Louisiana, 1982-84) with 8,326, and Jeff George (Warren Central, Indiana, 1983-85), with 8,126, had thrown more yardage during their high school careers.

Ty's 8,005 yards comfortably put him ahead of six other players on the Top 10 list of passers and knocked Mark Rypien of Spokane, Washington's Shadle Park High down to No. 11. The other six on the Top 10 list included (in order behind Ty) Saul Graves (Monroe,

Louisiana), Pat Haden (Bishop, California), Jim Plum (Helix, California), Joe Ferguson (Shreveport, Louisiana), and Dan McGwire (Claremont, California).

It's perhaps interesting to note that during Ty's senior collegiate year, when he threw for more than 15,000 yards at BYU, Mark Rypien led the Washington Redskins to a win over Buffalo in Super Bowl XXVI.

E. C. Lee remembers Sonny Detmer as a brilliant genius of an offensive football coach. "It was unbelievable. You'd hear him talking about offensive sets and plays and he'd be rattling it off so fast you couldn't understand what he was talking about. He had the ability to know where all 22 players were on the field on every single play—all the time. Everybody would go bananas."

Lee said the key with Sonny's coaching of Ty was his emphasis on the brain, not brawn. On the way home from school, Sonny would talk about play situations with Ty. They'd talk about what to do, what to see, what to expect, how to react. "Sonny taught Ty to think 360 times a day instead of throw 360 passes in practice. Ty usually only threw 100 passes in practice; the rest of the time he was thinking and learning and Sonny was teaching and listening to Ty. Sonny taught Ty it is easier to outsmart a foe than to outmuscle him."

That was good news for Ty. At 6-0 and 150 pounds he didn't have a lot of muscle mass.

Under the leadership of Sonny Detmer, other sports teams made the playoffs for the first time ever. The girls did it in volleyball and basketball. The boys baseball team went to the playoffs in 1985 and 1986—the first time in 34 years.

The basketball team, with Reed helping Mike Harris (on staff before Sonny arrived), beat 15 ranked 5A teams and made the playoffs. Southwest was a smaller 4A team. In December 1986, Southwest played No. 1 5A Bryan High from College Station, Texas (Bryan was ranked No.1 in the state, both 1983 and 1984.) It was a Christmas tournament. Bryan was seeded No. 1 in the tournament; the Dragons were seeded No. 34. Behind a great first quarter by Ty, the Dragons jumped all over Bryan High, leading 18-2. With his team trailing the Dragons 40-15 in the second quarter, Bryan coach Larry Brown was so embarrassed he left the bench and sat in the stands. Ty made eight of the last nine points and Southwest won by 18.

Sonny Detmer loved the kids at Southwest. For many of them, it was a new experience. They'd had little to love about life and few adults to experience it with. After school, after practice, many of the players hung around Sonny. They didn't want to go home. Sonny loaded them up in his pickup truck and delivered them to their houses. It was hard to drive away.

In 1988 the school board which governs Southwest High School ordered Sonny Detmer reassigned and out of the football program. He refused and, in essence, was fired.

Sonny refuses to comment on the reasons why he ran into trouble. Some say it was his emphasis on the pass and Ty; others claim it was jealousy of his success and growing power. Still others say it boiled down to politics, which Texas football is famous for anyway. There are some rumors that Sonny stood up for some employees other people wanted fired.

"Sonny was dealt a bum deal," said E. C. Lee.

The Detmers left Texas in 1988 for the first time since Sonny and Betty brought one-year-old Ty to the land of his ancestors. Southwest High School has not had a playoff team in any sport since.

Ty Detmer, the most famous student to ever attend Southwest High School, has never set foot in that school again, and probably never will.

EIGHT

CHOOSING A COLLEGE— THE RECRUITING MYTH

It sounded good. It made good copy. But it was not exactly the truth. The real story of the recruiting of Ty Detmer has remained a hidden part of his otherwise well-known legend.

The popular story of Ty Detmer's college recruiting, chronicled by the press in various magazines and newspapers, goes something like this: Ty Detmer made a list of schools he wanted to go to. Then the summer before his senior year he hopped in the car with his family. The Detmers drove to Provo to see BYU on the way to UCLA. Ty loved Happy Valley and Provo. He committed to BYU on the spot, terminating the trip to UCLA. Ty moved from Texas to Camelot.

It's true that Ty decided his own fate. But there is a story behind the story.

First, there's a lot missing between the lines. Like a lifetime family friend named Neil Reed. And a brotherly friendship forged between Sonny Detmer and a rookie BYU assistant football coach named Claude Bassett, assigned to recruit Texas. Nobody ever wrote it up, nobody ever fully gave both men credit. But Neil Reed is the single most significant influence on Ty Detmer's coming to the campus of BYU.

In Texas, going out of state is no easy task. This is a place that abhors its native sons leaving the Lone Star State. They'd rather see their heroes swamped in the Pecos River than become Arkansas Hogs. They'd prefer their gladiators join a ballet touring company from Austin rather than escape to Oklahoma and play for those hated Sooners. For a Texan, even changing his license plates when venturing outside the hallowed Panhandle boundary is blasphemy. Who in the name of Tom Landry could do that? Thus, for a bonafide star like Ty to go to *Utah*? He might as well have hiked up the Andes and played a flute than descend among those Mormons.

Coach Neil Reed was not connected with BYU in any way (he'd never even been on campus). In fact, he emptied his pockets repeatedly promoting and searching for a college for Ty. It was Reed's unofficial commission from Sonny and Betty Detmer to find their son a place where he'd be happy, a place where he could play, a place where he could succeed, that set Neil looking.

Why would the Detmers put this in the hands of Neil Reed? Who *is* this guy?

Neil Reed first met Sonny Detmer when Sonny played sandlot football in Indiana at age 12. Reed served as the chief recruiter and right-hand man for the greatest basketball coach ever, the legendary Adolph Rupp at Kentucky. It was Reed who recruited All-American Pat Riley in the mid-'60s out of Schenectady, New York for Kentucky. Neil Reed had as much to do with little Louie Dampier becoming All-American as anybody outside Rupp. In the late '80s, Riley later coached the Los Angeles Lakers and Magic Johnson to a myriad of NBA championships.

Reed's contacts are nationwide. They include college people, professional athletes, federal judges, members of the media and even members of the U.S. Congress.

A man who gave up the big-time lights of college and professional coaching to spend time with high school kids so he could see his own children grow up, Reed's cumulative coaching record in basketball is 581-77. Mike Harris, former basketball coach at Southwest High, claims 85 percent of what he knows about basketball comes from Reed. "The other 15 percent I stole from others," he says. As a baseball coach in high school, junior high and American Legion when Legion baseball was end-all and be-all of the summer season, Reed's teams went 804-48. As a football coach his overall record is 56-7. He coached 14 national championship teams as well as 23 state champions in the three sports combined, including four national American Legion Junior Baseball championships. Reed knew coaching. And he knew talent.

Reed's coaching experiences took him to Indiana, Ohio, Kentucky, Louisiana, Illinois, southern California and Texas. He spent four years in Lexington with Rupp, helping assemble Rupp's Runts of 1966, which won 32 games that season.

Ron Brocato, a columnist for the *States-Item* in New Orleans, wrote in December 1973 of Reed: "To almost everyone who attends local high school basketball games Neil Reed is a nameless face in the crowd. But given time and proper conditions, he could be the man to revolutionize the game at the prep level. Reed, a mystery man of sorts, is a former Indiana high school star, whose odyssey in the basketball world is probably unparalleled.

"A former advisor to Adolph Rupp at Kentucky and John Wooden at UCLA.... he is a virtual encyclopedia of basketball in its most complex and simple forms. This is Neil Reed."

Rupp personally recommended and entrusted his beloved Kentucky basketball program to Neil Reed in a letter to the university board of control. Wrote Rupp, the winningest coach in NCAA history: "...I have never been associated with anyone, more certainly at his age, who has a greater knowledge or teaching ability.... He is the best coach in the business. Period!"

Athletes Reed impacted in his career include Pat Riley, Louie Dampier, Dan Issel, Roger Staubach, Isaac Curtis, Will Clark, Jimmy Wynn, David Meyers, Larry Conley, Tommy Kron, Carl Ward, Eddie Brinkman, Norm Anderson, Charles White, Cotton Nash, Robin

Freemen, Art Mahaffey, Jim Sturgeon, Jim Fassel, Sonny Detmer and his sons Ty and Koy.

Joe B. Hall eventually took over the reins at Kentucky. There are many in the Midwest who wonder what would have happened if Reed had succeeded Rupp. Would there have been a new name alongside North Carolina's Dean Smith or Arizona's Lute Olsen?

Disgusted by recruiting scandals in college, Reed turned all his attention to high school and junior high athletics. He currently lives in San Clemente, California.

As counselor, advisor, quasi-amateur agent and family friend, and a man who'd been around two Heisman winners in Staubach and White, Reed took on the business of ferreting out the truth and lies of the college recruiting maze for Sonny. Ty would ultimately make his own choice, but it would be made on the research and expertise of Reed's advice to Sonny and Ty both.

Reed believed in Ty. "God gave him a very special talent. I could see it even in the eighth and ninth grade. He'd be a great one. He had that special something that Larry Bird and all the great ones have."

E.C. Lee, who knew Ty and Reed during Ty's Pop Warner football playing days, says everybody knew Ty could play, but many doubted Ty could make it big in Division I football because he wasn't an overpowering muscle guy. "Even Sonny wondered exactly how Ty would fit in college," says Lee. "Neil Reed never wondered at all; he claimed he'd be great."

After Ty's junior year, Reed and Ty made a chart, listing key considerations for a major college. They included size of stadium, football tradition, coaching staff, climate, outdoor recreation (hunting and fishing), bowl possibilities, conference championship possibilities, quality of education and the cleanliness of the people (no guns and knives and campus killings).

Reed started making contacts. He called a former athlete of his, Norm Anderson (the wide receiver coach at UCLA), Jerry Hanlon (a coach at Michigan), people at Illinois where Coach Mike White was throwing the ball, Louisiana State University (in a state where Reed had coached in the Catholic League), and, of course, BYU.

The summer of 1986, Reed arranged the airline, motel and rental car reservations for himself, Sonny, Ty and Koy. The plan was to inspect the schools during a football tour.

Ty had seen BYU defeat Air Force and watched All-America quarterback Robbie Bosco execute the Cougar passing offense. Reed kept pushing BYU and Ty listened.

Reed's football tour itinerary called for the four of them to fly to Los Angeles, see UCLA, drive to Palo Alto, fly to BYU, and then fly to Chicago, where they'd drive to the University of Iowa in Iowa City. From there they'd drive to Champaign and see Illinois. The group would then drive to Ann Arbor and the University of

80

Michigan, near where Sonny's uncle lived. From there they'd fly to Birmingham, Alabama, get another rental car and drive to Ray Perkins at Alabama. Then they would drive to New Orleans and on to Baton Rouge to inspect Louisiana State University. From there they would drive to Reed's home in Kingwood, Texas outside Houston and catch a plane to San Antonio.

The airline tickets were non-refundable. The motel and car rental agreements were.

That summer the Detmers ended up packing and driving directly to Provo en route to UCLA. They never made it to Los Angeles or anywhere else. As it turned out, the entire recruiting scenario ended in Provo when Ty loved the campus, community and program so much he committed on the spot to LaVell Edwards.

"There really was nowhere else for Ty. BYU's situation and Ty were a perfect marriage," said Reed.

In the summer of 1985, BYU linebacker coach Claude Bassett had been in the office when he received a phone call from football secretary Shirley Johnson, who indicated there was a man named Neil Reed on the phone. Reed had talked to head coach LaVell Edwards before, but wanted to talk to a coach right then. Bassett was the only one in.

He picked up the phone and began what would be the first of hundreds of phone calls to Reed.

"Reed told me about Ty Detmer, that he'd be a junior that fall at Southwest High and he was pretty good,"

81

said Bassett. "He told me right there on the spot that Ty Detmer was All-America material."

Bassett, a rookie assistant coach who'd worked as a graduate assistant the previous year, was initially assigned to recruit California, where he'd had marginal success. Bassett asked Edwards if he would consider letting him recruit Texas. Previously, BYU did not make regular trips to the Lone Star State, but concentrated efforts in California and the Rocky Mountain area.

Edwards wanted to get more speed into BYU's defense. He agreed to open up Texas in 1986 and assigned Bassett to take the area.

"I kept getting these videos from Reed," said Bassett. "Sometimes he'd send film. I was fascinated watching Ty play. He was unbelievable."

In May 1986 Bassett took off for Texas. By this time Bassett and Reed had spoken at least a hundred times. They set up a meeting.

Bassett arrived in Texas on April 30 and immediately hit Odessa and Midland, then drove his rental car up Interstate 20 to Sweetwater and Abilene and San Angelo, making stops at as many high schools as he could. On Friday, May 2, he hit San Antonio and visited with D.W. Rutledge at Judson Converse. In time this school would yield the Cougars' all-conference performers Earl Kauffman and safety Derwin Gray. There was a track meet scheduled that afternoon at Northside Stadium and Bassett planned to meet Sonny Detmer for the first time.

Sonny happened to be on the phone talking to BYU offensive coordinator Roger French when Bassett arrived at Southwest that day.

Bassett first met Dragon assistant coach Bill Lehman in the football office in the fieldhouse. Bassett sat down in the office and Lehman put on a film of Ty. "I was in total shock," Bassett recalls. "Here was this quarterback ramming the ball past defensive backs who would end up at Texas and Oklahoma. He'd complete 22 of 24 passes and cut defenses to pieces."

After seeing the film, Bassett made his way out to the track where Sonny had come as soon as his phone call was over. A few minutes later he sat in the bleachers and visited with Sonny.

"It was one of the greatest afternoons I've ever had in my life," says Bassett. "I felt like I'd known him all my life. We talked football. We talked Ty. We talked BYU and the passing game. I was amazed at his knowledge of offensive football and he knew a lot about BYU and had plenty of questions."

Sonny invited Bassett to a barbecue at the school the following night and there Bassett first met Reed. "I met Ty for the first time that Saturday in the parking lot of the high school," says Bassett. "He struck me as a great kid, quiet, humble and nice-looking. We couldn't talk because of NCAA restrictions, but I heard him talking to Coach Reed."

Reed and Sonny asked Bassett if he'd speak at an athletic banquet later that month. Bassett worked it out so he could.

Nearly 60 days later, the Detmers were in Provo, visiting Coach Edwards, who terminated a visit to Santa Barbara to be there that July morning.

Ty and Sonny were looking at a BYU football camp practice drill when Ty suddenly told his father he was going to commit to BYU. He loved the campus and hunting and fishing were so close, he could almost do them between class breaks.

"Are you sure, Ty?" asked Sonny. "If you commit, that's it. There will be no trips, no other considerations. It will be over."

Ty looked at the mountains once again. "No, sir, I won't change my mind. I'll commit."

Sonny told Ty to go tell Edwards. He did.

"Ty never wavered in his commitment to go to BYU," said Bassett, who traveled to Southwest High six times that fall and watched the Dragons and Ty play as BYU's official representative. "Ty took a lot of flack that fall for his commitment to BYU. He had a rough season too, but he still threw for over 3,000 yards and broke all kinds of records. Ty was a pearl among the clams. He never broke his word. From that summer day until now he's been loyal and devoted to BYU, refusing to turn to the NFL after his Heisman year. He has been an outstanding representative of our university."

Bassett remembers it was a joke with the Detmers whenever Coach Edwards would call. Ty never said much on the phone. Or anywhere. "We had a standing laugh that when Coach Edwards called it would last a minute and a half and Edwards would do all the talking. About one minute, 30 seconds was the standard length," says Bassett.

Reflecting on the career of Ty Detmer, Bassett says the most sobering thought is that Ty absolutely breaks the mold.

"Everything about the kid breaks the mold. He is a trendsetter, a prototype of greatness, not only on the field but off. Ty is fiercely competitive. He knew exactly what he wanted out of the college experience, went after it and never looked back, second-guessing himself, his teammates or coaches. He is a natural leader and is tremendously loyal to the things which are important. You look into Ty's eyes on the football field and you know you are looking at a player. You feel it. There wasn't a time I was around him I didn't think he would be the greatest quarterback ever.

"Ty Detmer set a standard in college football that will never be equaled. I can bet you 50 years from now, people will still be talking about Ty Detmer, the most decorated player to ever play the game. Nobody's ever going to come close. It will be like Bob Beamon's long jump record that stood for decades.

"There is no doubt Ty's numbers will be in the NCAA record book forever. Every quarterback in the future of college will be measured by the benchmark set by Ty. I can't imagine anybody ever doing more for the game, giving more of his time, and performing on cue when you needed a play. His consistency is a legend."

NINE

REDSHIRT FRESHMAN— HELP WANTED

There is no place on the planet like Provo, Utah. Nestled at the foothills of the Wasatch Mountain range on the east, the city sits at an elevation of 4,500 feet. Utah Lake is on its western boundaries, while the majestic snow-tipped peak of Mt. Timpanogos is framed in the pressbox windows of 65,000-seat Cougar Stadium.

Provo receives the full palette of four changing seasons. Its close mountain canyons, thick with quakies and pine, hide adequate herds of elk and mule deer. Marshy wetlands and rural fields are home to flocks of ducks, geese and pheasants. The Provo River, a blue-ribbon brown trout fishery, winds its way through Provo Canyon. One fork fingers its way from the base of actor Robert Redford's estate and Sundance ski resort, all just minutes from the campus of Brigham Young University.

The average age of the population of Utah Valley is 22. The state leads the nation in consumption of ice cream. Many refer to Utah County as "Happy Valley." Fans of the Mormon Church-sponsored Brigham Young

University take their football program seriously. More than 10,000 travel from Salt Lake City, 45 miles north on Interstate 15, and from as far away as Idaho, to home games. Provo is the seat of Utah County, population 250,000. Followers of Cougar football see the team as an extension of themselves.

BYU fans have somewhat of an inferiority complex, a below-the-skin persecution complex if you will. They feel they are not taken seriously or respected. This may date back to their pioneer ancestors—a people driven from New York, Ohio, Illinois and Missouri, many of them destined to walk across a continent before helping to create and nurture new settlements in the West. To remedy this urge for acceptance, today's fans subconsciously look to BYU's athletic programs to stand as their proxy in the battle for an equal regard. They see the football program as warrior with shining sword, swatting irreverent gentiles in time to the time-honored litany of the underdog: "Take THAT. *Respect* us. *Recognize* us!"

BYU fans eagerly await recognition in national magazines or validation by national sportscasters, and they take great pride when BYU's football and basketball teams achieve Top 25 rankings. It's as if they, personally, have been stamped with a seal of approval. No fans watch rankings more closely than those at BYU.

In this setting, the fans swallow up victories like a kid downs Hershey's kisses. Their football heroes, particularly quarterbacks, are exalted above what is realistically normal for mere players of a game. Such fans also take losses very personally. After a loss they are pained to the core and often look for a whipping boy. Blame goes to a quarterback or whomever is choosing the quarterback in Provo if he loses. Deep is the pit he is thrown into if he fails.

This, in a nutshell, is the local neighborhood of BYU's powerhouse Quarterback Factory.

And it is on this stage a quarterback in Provo must perform. On this stage BYU needed serious help the year Detmer left Texas for BYU. His first season in Provo (1987), Detmer redshirted. (A redshirt signifies a player who is attending school, but is taking the year off from playing. The NCAA allows a player five years to complete four years of eligibility.)

The man credited with the success of BYU football since 1972 is LaVell Edwards. It is his job to nurse BYU fans and their egos with wins. Edwards, a likable and stone-faced veteran coach, is the former president of the College Football Association. He pioneered the establishment of a traveling retirement program for his profession. Popular with his peers and the media nationwide, Edwards won the mythical national college football championship in 1984 and ranks among active coaches as having the third highest percentage of wins.

After an unprecedented chain of consecutive Western Athletic Conference football championships (10 between 1975 and 1985), Cougar football ranked third behind Miami and Nebraska as one of the most successful football programs of the '80s. But because of a drought of quarterbacks and some lean recruiting years after the 1984 national championship, BYU found itself dethroned from its lofty WAC perch.

In 1985 upstart 10-1 Air Force Academy with its precision wishbone attack tied 11-3 BYU for the conference title. It was the final year for All-America quarterback Robbie Bosco. The Cougars lost to Ohio State 10-7 in the Citrus Bowl.

In 1986, "Quarterback U" suddenly hit the skids. Lots of schools, *especially* in the WAC, would welcome a record of 8-5, 9-4 and 9-4 (a combined three-year record of 26-13), but at BYU, it was considered a problem. In Provo it wasn't so much the record of those three years that shook up the natives. It was the lack of winning championships three years running and the absence of flame-throwing quarterbacks to lead the Cougars' high-octane offense. It made for an un-Happy Valley.

At the end of each of three "non-champion" seasons, the quarterback on the field was not the same one who started that season's first game. After placing a quarterback on the All-WAC team eight of the previous nine years, in 1986, 1987 or 1988 BYU quarterbacks failed to make the All-WAC team. For 10 consecutive years the quarterback position at BYU produced an annual average of 3,000-yards in passing. During the three post-Bosco years, no quarterback cracked the 3,000-yard standard.

In a nutshell, the Quarterback Factory was in recession.

Steve Lindsley first took the reins as quarterback in 1986. The former Ricks Junior College All-American from Skyline High in Salt Lake City threw for 2,247 yards. In the Cougars' final game of the year against UCLA in the Freedom Bowl, Lindsley stood on the sidelines. His replacement, Bob Jensen, faced the Bruins and swallowed a 31-10 loss. No WAC title.

Bob Jensen started in 1987. A big, strong, powerfully-built athlete from Fillmore, Utah, Jensen lasted nine games. When BYU ended that season, losing to Virginia 22-16 in the All-American Bowl, the quarterback was Provo's own Sean Covey. Jensen quit the team, forfeiting his senior year of eligibility for a chance at Canadian professional football. It didn't last. (On the sidelines that season was redshirt Ty Detmer.) No WAC title.

Covey started the 1988 season at Wyoming on national television. The nation watched Wyoming whip BYU 24-14 that night. But they also got their first look at Ty Detmer. A Wyoming blitz knocked Covey out. Literally. Detmer the freshman ran onto the field. He threw a touchdown pass to Chuck Cutler on his first drive. Then Wyoming, tasting blood, smothered the rookie. Wyoming sacked Detmer five times and intercepted him four times. Detmer completed just 9 of 26 passes. "Making the step up from high school to that game was a big jump. I learned something that night.

Everything is quicker. Even from working out in a scrimmage, this was a faster game," said Ty.

Covey returned and led the Cougars to an impressive 46-6 win over Texas and 31-18 decision over TCU. But seven times in 1988 Detmer came in as relief because of Covey's injuries or ineffectiveness.

After the Texas win, BYU's record was 1-1. The Cougars then faced another WAC foe—UTEP—in Provo, September 17. The Cougars could not afford another league loss if they were to be in contention for the title. Covey put the Cougars ahead 17-3 with a 15-yard pass to Chuck Cutler and a 66-yarder to Jeff Frandsen. Then with seven minutes to play in the first half, that lead evaporated. UTEP scored, then received a gift. Covey threw a pass which Miner defender Richie Wright intercepted and returned 72 yards for a touchdown. Another Covey interception set up the Miners inside BYU's 10-yard line, where they easily scored again. UTEP racked up 21 points in seven minutes. BYU, once in control 17-3, left the field at intermission, behind 24-17.

The BYU players were shell-shocked. The coaches were stunned. No WAC title in two years and now the Cougars were getting their butts kicked like at Wyoming. And the offense had just handed UTEP 14 points. An unforgiving Provo crowd, known for booing quarterbacks, wondered exactly what reception to give Covey. Hometown kid or not, Covey, the hero of the Texas game (323 yards and two touchdowns), found himself on smoldering coals. He'd thrown for 361 yards on the Miners in one half. But his two picks erased the board. BYU was behind.

During intermission, Edwards told Detmer he would start the second half. Detmer began spring practice expecting to play behind Jensen and Covey. When Jensen quit, he was happy to be the backup. Now just three games into the season he'd be thrown into a battle like that with Wyoming. They would give him the reins. Rookie or not, Detmer was determined this day would be no Wyoming night. All he wanted was the chance.

Detmer was unable to mount a scoring drive in the third quarter. BYU's defense limited the Miners to just one field goal the rest of the game. UTEP led 27-17 when the fourth quarter began. Tension mounted. It made the next 15 minutes very dramatic.

Cougar strong safety Troy Long intercepted two Miner passes to squelch the Miner offense. BYU's defense became more determined to prove that the cause was not lost. Detmer mounted one short scoring drive, hitting Cutler on a third and long to keep the drive alive. After the score BYU trailed 27-24. But time was running out. With four minutes left in the game Detmer dropped back, looked, waited, then spotted fullback Fred Whittingham clearing himself in the end zone. The fullback was the second option receiver on the play, but was left wide open by the Miners, who had covered BYU's wideouts. Detmer zipped the football to Whittingham, who caught it just over his head for the winning touchdown. Detmer was 1-0 as a reliever. In the locker room the team mood had spun 180 degrees from that at halftime. Reporters gathered around Detmer wanting details of that touchdown pass. Nearby, Covey dressed. His heart was in his shoes. Two high-ranking school officials, dressed in suits, entered the locker room and made their way to Covey, shaking his hand and patting him on the back. Detmer with reporters, Covey with men in suits, teammates celebrating. It was a scene.

Whether he wanted it or not, Edwards was once again in a quarterback controversy. It had not yet blossomed, but the seeds were planted. His coaching staff and players were starting to divide themselves over the issue of who should be starting. The fans had enough fodder from the UTEP game to fuel them at barbershops and lunch breaks all season.

Covey returned to lead the Cougars to impressive wins over Utah State 38-3, Colorado State 42-7 and Texas Christian 31-18. All appeared well in Happy Valley. The Cougars were a respectable 5-1 and had no reason to believe they wouldn't win the WAC title.

On October 22, 1988 the Cougars made their annual trek to Hawaii. The road trip is the longest league trip in college football. Before 50,000 spectators in Aloha Stadium, Covey led BYU to a 17-3 lead. Despite fumbling a few snaps, Covey's performance was solid enough for victory, but then the Provoan went down with a knee injury. Detmer came in as relief. Playing past midnight (Utah time), Hawaii made a furious rally in the second half, scoring 21 points. The Rainbow Warriors, who hate BYU, started in on Detmer. With six minutes to play in the game, Hawaii came after Ty with an eight-man blitz. Detmer spotted Chuck Cutler coming across the middle and pegged him with a 24-yard pass. Cutler took the ball, turned upfield, and completed a 71-yard touchdown pass play. It proved to be the game winner. BYU won 24-23. Detmer was 2-0 as a reliever.

Covey was unable to start the following week. Sonny and Koy drove to Provo for Ty's first start of his career. BYU climbed into the national rankings for the first time since 1986. Working out full-time with the first unit offense for the first time made a big difference for Detmer. "I felt very comfortable all week long. I was ready. New Mexico wasn't exactly a powerhouse, but it was a conference game and we had to get it," said Detmer. That day BYU won 65-0. Detmer completed 24 of 35 passes for 333 yards and five touchdowns with no interceptions. Detmer was 3-0 as a reliever-starter.

The next week BYU lost all hopes for a WAC title, losing to San Diego State 27-15. Covey started the game, but left due to injury. Then he returned to finish the game. The Cougars whipped Air Force 48-31 behind Covey the next week. It was the last win of the regular season. BYU would end the year with losses to Utah (57-28) and Miami (41-17). In both of those, Detmer would finish the game.

95

At the Utah confrontation, a Covey pass was intercepted by a lineman just three feet after it left Covey's hands. It went for a touchdown and Utah led 21-0. On the sidelines, Matt Bellini went berserk. Utah, which hadn't defeated BYU in 10 years, kicked the tar out of the Cougars and knocked Covey out of the game. One particular sack of Covey in this game became a motif, a piece of artwork used by University of Utah promotions and marketing departments over the next two seasons. Pieces of the goal posts were made into ashtrays and paperweights and sold to Ute boosters.

Covey's performance was not the sole reason BYU lost to Utah. But the BYU offense had eight turnovers. Quarterbacks get the praise in wins and the blame in losses. The Cougar defense had little clue how to stop Utah's quarterback Scott Mitchell.

Ever since the Hawaii game, both offensive and defensive players came to Detmer, praising his leadership on the field. Said one player: "Sean is a good friend of mine and I like him, but you are the better quarterback." In this atmosphere, the Cougars limped to their closing game of the season (at Miami) and left with a season record of 8-4. The Freedom Bowl Committee had extended an invitation to BYU to play Colorado the day of the Utah game. But believe it, they probably had second thoughts.

Detmer would replace Covey for the last time at the Freedom Bowl in Anaheim on December 29, 1988.

Cutler, BYU's leading receiver that year, caught nine touchdowns in 1988, eight from Detmer.

Covey started against Colorado in the Freedom Bowl, but the MVP Trophy went to Detmer, who led the Cougars to a 20-17 victory over the Buffs. It was BYU's first bowl victory in four years. For the third consecutive season, the quarterback who started the first game of the year was on the sidelines at the end of December. No WAC title.

That night in Anaheim culminated a perplexing and stormy era of LaVell Edwards' career. What had happened to BYU's offense? What was the deal with the quarterbacks? Why no league titles? Sure, BYU came close, but the WAC was not exactly the Big 10, Big 8 or Pac 10.

In 1988, Edwards remained loyal to Covey. The Provoan was not only a local, but his parents were next-door neighbors to Edwards. Lindsley and Jensen both left the BYU program with fans thinking they were somehow failures. They were outstanding young men. None deserved to be labeled as failures. Edwards gave Covey the chance to start every game he was physically able to. Sean worked hard; he was loyal. Edwards would not leave Covey to the wolves, a pack BYU fans sometimes became.

ABC commentator Keith Jackson said of Edwards: "LaVell Edwards is successful because he is a better man than he is a football coach. And he is a damn good coach." Edwards would not trash Sean Covey or any player.

One person who took a heap of criticism during this 36-month period was quarterback-receiver coach Norm Chow. He got it from letter writers, on radio call-in shows and from the stands. Chow became the favorite goat. Frustrated after the 1988 campaign, Chow told Edwards if he wanted his resignation, he could have it.

One popular theory circulating was that Edwards needed a quarterback coach who'd played quarterback. Chow was an all-conference lineman at the University of Utah. Edwards assigned him joint quarterback and receiver duty when Mike Holmgren left Provo for the San Francisco '49ers. Holmgren had replaced Ted Tollner, who took the head job at Southern California. Tollner replaced Doug Scovil, who took the head job at San Diego State, then turned to the NFL.

Lindsley, Jensen and Covey were all successful high school quarterbacks. They appeared to have the skills to get the job done. Because BYU's recruiting came up short in some ways at this time, these three may not have had the supporting cast their famous predecessors worked with. One common thread with all three was that they left their recruiting classes, football practices and school tasks to serve two-year volunteer missions for their church. They were all leaders. But as it should be, after their missions their priorities changed. Football became part of their world, but not their whole world. But to Ty, whose whole world was football, the sole focus was on how best to get that ball into the end zone. One receiver who played with all three of Ty's predecessors observed that BYU's plays started out well, but when the play broke down, other options (meaning play-saving improvisations on the part of the quarterback) just didn't happen, at least not consistently. Too often for Lindsley, Jensen and Covey, if BYU fell behind in a game, that game was over.

Meanwhile Detmer, an avid outdoorsman, was learning about Provo. He'd already shot his deer, elk, pheasant, dove and duck. He had staked out his favorite fishing holes on the Provo and Diamond Fork rivers. His redshirt year he traveled with the team. He even got to go to Australia when the Cougars played Colorado State in the final regular season game at the invitation of the folks down under.

Detmer was living a dream and just waiting his turn. He had everything he wanted from college life except enough football, his first love.

The first fall practice Detmer attended, in August of 1987, fresh out of Southwest High School, Norm Chow watched the Texan carefully. After practice Chow told Edwards, "We're back in the quarterback business."

As that autumn of 1987 progressed, it was decided Detmer would be saved for a rainy day, that he would redshirt because the Cougars had Jensen and Covey. The way it looked, Detmer would get just two complete years as a starter. That was all he expected. Even so, after one frustrating practice session, offensive coordinator Roger French complained one day, "We have only one guy out there who knows what's going on and he can't play because he's redshirting."

A rainy day came sooner than expected. Covey missed spring practice in March 1989 recovering from major knee surgery. He worked hard all summer and never missed a practice session all fall. But he'd left a crack in the door for Detmer. That was all the lanky Texan needed.

After one week of practice in August 1989, Edwards walked up to Detmer as he was leaving the practice field. That very week his teammates had voted him the first sophomore captain in school history. "You'll be the starter in the opener at New Mexico," said Edwards.

"O.K., Sir," nodded Detmer.

There were no bells or whistles. No press conference was scheduled. The band was nowhere near.

But that August day under the peaks of Mt. Timpanogos the Detmer Era began. In the end it brought back enough manna to feed the starved Cougar faithful. Among Ty Detmer's successes: three All-America quarterback citations, three MVP bowl designations, a Heisman Trophy, 59 NCAA records, and 15,000-plus yards.

And, lest anyone forget, three WAC titles in a row.

Following the final Detmer appearance in Provo (a 48-17 thumping of in-state rival Utah on November 23, 1991), H.B. Arnett, the publisher of *Cougar Sportsline*, a private newsletter subscribed to by BYU fans, concluded:

From our vantage point, the poignant moment of last Saturday afternoon wasn't the thumping of Utah, but the conclusion to Ty Detmer's career. If you are a BYU football fan you may want to ponder exactly what Detmer has meant to the Cougar football program. Basically, he singlehandedly saved BYU from sinking further into football mediocrity upon his arrival in Provo five years ago. In case you forgot what Detmer has meant to BYU football, when he arrived, the Cougars were in the midst of a three-year WAC-title losing streak and struggling to find a Division I quarterback.

Not only had BYU lost its magic with the pass, fans and media alike were even beginning to question the leadership of LaVell Edwards.... All Detmer did was refocus the college football world back on Provo with his offensive heroics and Heisman Trophy. BYU has had some pretty good football players during the last five years along with Detmer, but realistically speaking, without Ty Detmer at the quarterback helm for BYU, the Cougars would not have won the WAC crown this year or the last two seasons. It is that simple.

As simple as a Happy Valley Cougar fan in the land of ice cream and legendary quarterbacks.

TEN

THE SOPHOMORE WONDERBOY— WELCOME TO TY-LAND

In 1986 Claude Bassett and Neil Reed were eating Mexican food in San Antonio the season Ty Detmer finished his career at Southwest High School.

If there were ever an Olympic competition for story-telling, or good old yarn weaving, this twosome would share the gold medal. They could make parables out of every topic imaginable, from sports to federal government waste of EPA equipment on off-shore oil wells near Galveston. They could take a single football play and dissect it from the play-call and huddle to the whistle. They could give a four-second football play a plot, climax and resolution and spend 30 minutes filling in the blank spots. Put Sonny Detmer with these two and plan for an afternoon. AT&T has made a small fortune off Sonny, Neil and Claude. They should be shareholders in Mountain and Southwest Bell.

Neil is a walking encyclopedia. Sonny adds Paul Harvey commentary. Claude is James Michener. Their favorite topic is Ty.

At lunch that day, Bassett and Reed exchanged plot lines on Ty's future career at BYU. Nobody knows how many tacos they ate. But believe it, the waitress made off like a bandit with tips.

Reed made a prediction. Based on mathematics, equations and formulas he'd plotted on a napkin, he forecast that Ty would become college football's all-time leading passer. The key factor was Ty's yards per attempted pass. Reed based his prediction on the attempts generated by BYU quarterbacks Jim McMahon, Steve Young, and Robbie Bosco. At Southwest, Ty's yardage per attempt hovered around 10.5 yards. His yards per completion ranked even higher. In 1986, he set the national high school record by averaging 335.4 yards per game.

"If he gets more than two years at BYU, he'll do enough to break McMahon's NCAA passing record for total yardage and will get his efficiency mark too," claimed Reed.

McMahon's six-year-old NCAA record of 9,433 career yards was still the NCAA standard. So was his 4,571 for a single season. (McMahon's 9,433 would later be surpassed by Todd Santos, Doug Flutie and others.)

Bassett reminded Reed that BYU had Bob Jensen and Sean Covey and if they played out their careers, Ty would have only two seasons.

"Well, you guys have nobody who can match Ty," said Reed. "Nobody. And you know it. And if Ty gets just two years, he'd be over 10,000. He will do everything necessary to win a Heisman Trophy; whether they give it to him is another matter."

This conversation became key to the 1989 football season in Provo. Cougar fans were hungry for a quarterback—a guy who could lead them back to the glory days of McMahon, Young and Bosco. This was the sophomore year for Ty. It was his first year as a starting college quarterback. In many ways it was the finest season of his career. Cougar fans had their hero. Provo became Ty-Land with Ty-lites on TV stations, Ty-lines in newspapers and a video called the Tysman Rap. Reed was on his way to becoming a prophet.

In 1989, BYU went 10-3 and won the WAC football title for the first time in three years. One trademark of Ty's passing was his insistence on pushing the ball downfield. He liked to challenge an opponent's safeties by throwing post patterns. The trouble was that BYU's receivers seldom had enough speed to attack a post pattern and break it open. And Ty did not have the patience to just let it go. Against Washington State that year, Ty drove BYU into scoring position twice. He then forced two passes which were intercepted, killing both drives. BYU lost the game 46-41. The only other BYU loss of the regular season came at Hawaii, three time zones away, a 56-14 thumping.

BYU's 1989 wins included a 24-3 victory at New Mexico, a 31-10 whipping of Navy in Annapolis, a 37-10 pasting of Utah State, a 36-20 victory over defending WAC champion Wyoming, a 45-16 win at Colorado State, a 49-24 decision over UTEP, a 44-35 shootout with Air Force, a 70-31 payback to Utah and a 48-27 win at San Diego State.

Ty set more than a dozen NCAA passing records during the season. Houston's Ware also put up incredible numbers. The two Texans were the talk of college football. Ware had his run-and-shoot offense clicking for the Houston Cougars. Detmer had ignited the fire in his Cougar offensive machine. The big difference in the two was the number of throws. Ware was throwing every time he could possibly throw; Ty was balancing out BYU's attack with a mixture of the pass and run. Ware won the Heisman Trophy in 1989. But the statistical formula etched out on a napkin by Reed two years before struck a resounding chord. Ty Detmer was incredible.

Based on Ty's high school stats, Reed estimated Ty would average 10.5 yards per *attempt*. In 1989 Ty broke McMahon's 10-year-old NCAA record by averaging 11.07 per attempt (McMahon's mark was 10.27). Ty also broke the record for yards per *completion* by averaging 17.2 (McMahon's 10-year-old standard was 16.1).

"So I was off half a yard per attempt," chuckled Reed. "Still McMahon and Ty are the only two college quarterbacks to average more than 10 yards per

106

attempt and that says a lot for BYU's offensive scheme. That is a big, big key when looking at quarterback statistics. It shows how efficiently BYU can throw the football."

When it comes to quarterbacking, the NCAA "passing efficiency rating" says it all. The rating is based on a complicated formula used to provide a simple picture of which quarterback moves the football the most effectively. It is fair to the guys who throw hundreds of passes. It is fair to quarterbacks who toss only 50 or 70 in a season. It exposes what you do with the football.

In that formula, one key ingredient is how many yards a quarterback throws per attempt.

In 1989, Ware broke McMahon's NCAA single season passing mark by 128 yards, throwing for 4,699. Ty had 4,560. But the totals are misleading unless the formula for efficiency is applied. Ware threw 578 passes; Ty tossed 412. Ware completed 365; Ty's receivers caught 265. But Detmer's yards per attempt averaged 11.07 to Ware's 8.13. Detmer's yards per completion set an NCAA mark of 17.21; Ware's settled in at 12.87. Ware's passing efficiency ranked 17th among the top 20 passers at 152.5. Ty led the nation in passing that year with a rating of 175.6. It was one-tenth off McMahon's single season NCAA record, set in 1980.

What does it all mean? Well, statistical mumbo jumbo aside, if Detmer had had Ware's attempts that year, Ty would have thrown for an astounding 6,398 yards! If Ware had taken Detmer's attempts, the 1989 Heisman Trophy winner would have thrown for only 3,349 yards.

Playing with statistics may prove moot. But in 1989, Detmer's performance in the books dominated that of his peers.

Interestingly enough, the Indianapolis Colts drafted Illinois quarterback Jeff George No. 1 in the subsequent NFL draft. The Colts signed the junior from Indiana for six years at $15 million. Remember Ty's rating of 175.6? George's passing efficiency rating in 1989 was 131.1. In the fall of 1990 *USA Today* highlighted Detmer as the leading candidate for the Heisman Trophy. Wrote Steve Wieberg in *USA Today*: "Detmer doesn't have George's strong right arm, but he's loaded with savvy and other Joe Montana-like intangibles, and his statistics through three games dwarf George's from a year ago."

The *USA Today*'s comparison of George and Detmer (using the first five games of their junior years as basis) reveals the following:

Completion rate: Detmer 68.6 percent, George 62.1
Yards per game: Detmer 413.7, George 209.7
Yards per attempt: Detmer 8.3, George 6.95
Touchdown passes per game: Detmer 3.0, George 1.7
Efficiency rating: Detmer 151.3, George 132.1

In the final game of 1989, the Cougars faced Penn State's Nittany Lions, winner of the Lambert Trophy (signifying that the team was the best in the East). The stage was Holiday Bowl XII in Jack Murphy Stadium, December 29. Joe Paterno's Nittany Lions were ranked 14th by UPI and 15th by Associated Press. The Cougars were 18th and 22nd.

That night Detmer threw for a major bowl record of 576 yards, shredding the Nittany Lion defense. Although the Cougars lost 50-39, BYU was unstoppable until the final scores. In the final three minutes, Paterno's team thwarted the Cougars in two key plays. (One PSU stop came when linebacker Andre Collins took the football out of Ty's cocked right arm and ran for a touchdown.) The broadcast of that Holiday Bowl was the highest-rated ESPN college football game in the cable network's history. "Nobody ever had a game like that on us. Nobody," said Paterno.

Nobody ever had a sophomore year like Detmer did in 1989. He threw for 4,560 yards (a hairs-breadth from McMahon's 1981 record of 4,571 yards, and not very far from Ware's first-place total of 4,699 yards the same year). He accounted for 32 touchdowns and completed 64 percent of his pass attempts, rising, as previously noted, to within 1/10th of one percent of McMahon's NCAA season passing efficiency record. The season had something for everybody. BYU fans had a new quarterback hero to dote over. Thanks to the ESPN exposure Detmer got against Penn State, college football had a marquee player. BYU football finally had a WAC title after a three-year wait. LaVell Edwards and his

109

staff didn't feel any heat. Letters and radio callers were pacified. And Neil Reed's napkin formula proved him a prophet.

In the final game of the 1989 season, Sonny loaded the family up in the van and drove 23 hours straight to see Ty's game against San Diego State. Ty needed 338 yards to break the existing single-season passing mark set by McMahon in 1980. Sonny wanted to see him break it.

The Cougars romped over the Aztecs. Five minutes into the fourth quarter, the Cougar offense was closing in on a 300-yard passing night for their young team captain. SDSU turnovers had placed BYU in great field position all night, cutting down the length of BYU scoring drives.

The game came at a time when both universities were trying to mend relationships. The previous year SDSU's All-WAC quarterback Todd Santos, a Mormon from Fresno, broke the NCAA career passing record in Cougar Stadium. Through a misunderstanding between SDSU athletic director Fred Miller and BYU officials, there was no formal recognition of the accomplishment. The Aztecs expected the game to be stopped and Santos given the game ball. BYU officials didn't like that scenario because, in 1986, a game in Provo was halted to honor Colorado State player Steve Bartolo (the Ram fullback broke the WAC rushing record). BYU felt the interruption cost the Cougars momentum: Bartolo demolished the Cougar defense during a game-winning last-minute drive. BYU lost to CSU 24-20. So on this night in 1989 at Jack Murphy Stadium, the question became one of diplomacy. After the Todd Santos incident, BYU flew a university vice president to San Diego with the game ball and an official apology but feelings still ran high.

What does all that have to do with this last game of 1989 and Ty's record? Maybe nothing, but it is background. Detmer passed for 326 yards that night, missing by only 11 the total yardage of 4,571 to tie McMahon's single-season NCAA passing record—with only 12 more yards Detmer could have become BYU's all-time leading passer.

Easily winning the game, BYU ran down the clock. No plays: just a safe win. Ironically, for a guy who averaged 11.07 per attempted pass, one more pass would have done the job. LaVell Edwards insisted afterwards he had no idea there was a record to be plucked. Norm Chow, responsible for play-calling, agreed. Chow, like some of his predecessors, had been known to call pass plays to help quarterbacks along. "I didn't know what he needed," said Chow afterwards.

Sonny Detmer left for Texas immediately after the game, less than pleased over what did and didn't happen. He drove all night long and dozed off at the wheel somewhere in the desert, skidding to a halt in the middle of nowhere. Betty and the kids were asleep in the back. They all could have been killed. When Sonny gassed up at the next stop, he checked the van over.

Stuck to the radiator was a clump of sagebrush and a dead bird.

"Boy," he said, "that was some night."

Coach Neil Reed, friend and
Ty supporter

Ty, age one, giving his Heisman smile

Ty (black hat) with spurs and boots

Fall 1962,
Sonny (All-America),
Betty (Homecoming Queen)

Ty with Betty
and Sonny

Johnny Unitas
pose in 1977

Photo Page 2

Ty during fourth grade YMCA game

Ty even kicked off, here in fifth grade YMCA game

At the plate as a Dragon,
Ty drew and blew fire

Posing as the Texas Player
of the Year in 1985

At Southwest, Ty excelled
in basketball

In New York at the Heisman ceremonies (from left) Betty, Lori, Kim and Dee

Sonny, Betty, Koy, Lori and Dee await the Heisman announcement in 1990
before Mission High playoff game in Kingsville

BYU Athletic Director Glen Tuckett (left) and LaVell Edwards celebrate
Heisman announcement at a Honolulu hotel, December 1, 1990

Doris and Hubert (Maw Maw and Paw Paw) Detmer, decked out in BYU
attire, celebrate the December 1, 1990 announcement on TV of grandson Ty's
Heisman *(Photo Copyright Express-News Corp., Used with permission)*

Photo Page 6

At the Davey O'Brien ceremonies (1992) in Fort Worth, Texas
(from left) LaVell Edwards, Kim, Ty, Sonny and Betty

BYU Davey O'Brien winners, (from left) Steve Young, Ty Detmer,
Jim McMahon and LaVell Edwards

Ty Detmer flinging passes during two-a-days in 1990 *(David Dahl photo)*

Just weeks before BYU defeated No. 1 Miami, Ty enjoys two-a-day practice session *(David Dahl photo)*

Just how skinny can Ty get? Look at him sideways *(David Dahl photo)*

The Detmer release which reminds many of Johnny Unitas *(Pat Krohn photo)*

Always the leader, Ty guides receivers into the open
(Mark Philbrick photo)

Photo Page 10

Scoring on a bootleg option run gainst Utah, November 23, 1991
(Jason Olsen Photo)

Matt Bellini receives a 23-year-old game ball from Phil Odle. Bellini broke
Odle's all-time receiving record at BYU in 1990 against Oregon
(David Dahl photo)

Sonny Detmer visits with Cougar Assistant Coach Claude Bassett before 1991
Holiday Bowl in San Diego *(Mark Philbrick photo)*

Photo Page 12

Chris Smith, talented two-time
All-America tight end,
never made it in the NFL
(Mark Philbrick Photo)

Ty looks over Utah's defense,
November 17, 1990
(Brian Tregaskis photo)

Audibilizing, Ty sets up a passing
route for BYU wide receivers
(Mark Philbrick photo)

A classic drop-back artist, Ty's
footwork represented solid
fundamental technique
(Mark Philbrick photo)

A Post-game smile from Ty after the 1991 ESPN game with San Diego State—A 52-52 tie (Mark Philbrick photo)

Kim and Ty pose for a 1991 promotional photo for use in a poster (Mark Philbrick photo)

Reporters from all over the country meet with Ty in a press conference following upset of Miami September 8, 1990. Note bandaged chin. Just moments before Ty and Sonny "giggled" over the phone (Mark Philbrick photo)

BYU trainer T.J. Byrne attends to Ty's cut chin during the nationally televised Miami upset *(Mark Philbrick photo)*

BYU fans flood the field in Cougar stadium after BYU's upset of No. 1 Miami, September 8 *(Mark Philbrick photo)*

Photo Page 15

Betty Detmer, wearing a Heisman tie of her own, during game at UTEP in the
Sun Bowl Stadium in 1990 *(Mark Philbrick photo)*

Photo Page 16

Betty and Ty pose before 1990 season opening game at UTEP
(Mark Philbrick photo)

Scrambling for his life Ty avoids Texas A&M pass rushers who wanted a
Heisman winner for dinner in 1990 Holiday Bowl
(Mark Philbrick photo)

Kim and Ty bag pheasants at an Orem, Utah, shooting club, March 17, 1992
(Rod Collett photo)

Utah Governor Norm Bangerter caches in on Tysmania in Utah December 1990
in autograph session *(Mark Philbrick photo)*

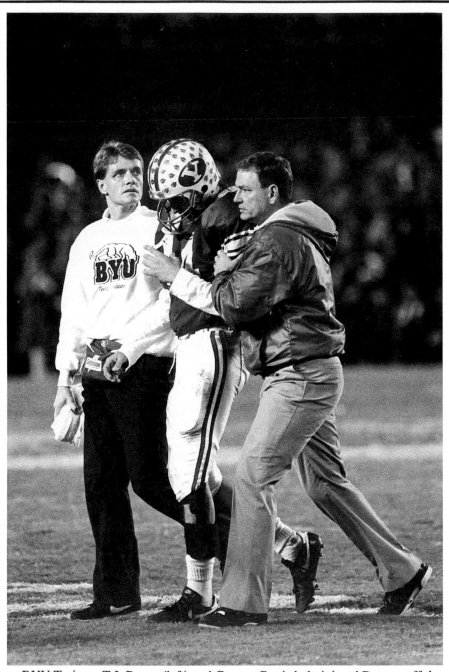

BYU Trainers T.J. Byrne (left) and George Curtis help injured Detmer off the
field in the 1990 Holiday Bowl. This was Detmer's only failure to finish a game
in his life *(Mark Philbrick photo)*

ESPN got its moneys worth in prime time performer Ty Detmer, interviewed here after the 1991 Holiday Bowl 13-13 tie with Iowa
(Mark Philbrick photo)

The celebration scene in Honolulu, December 1, 1990, when the Heisman announcement was made on national television. On Ty's right is Athletic Director Glen Tuckett, on Ty's left is Lavell Edwards. Behind, from left is BYU President Rex Lee, Chris Smith, Bryan May and David Henderson

(Mark Philbrick photo)

Photo Page 22

With two separated shoulders, Ty could barely lift the bronze Heisman,
but he had the pose down
(Mark Philbrick photo)

Ty's final appearance before the student body in the Marriott Center,
February 1992 *(Pat Krohn photo)*

Teammates say Good-bye to Ty Detmer after his final home game in Cougar
Stadium, November 23, 1991.
(Pat Krohn photo)

ELEVEN

BYU'S RECEIVERS: CATCHING EVERYTHING BUT THE NFL

Penn State coach Joe Paterno is a legend in college football and certainly knows talent when he sees it.

On December 29, 1989 his Nittany Lions were victorious against the Cougars, but Ty racked up 576 yards on the Penn State team before losing to them 50-39. Two years later on September 21, 1991, Penn State beat up on Detmer again, and his much younger and less experienced team, trouncing the Cougars 33-7 and sacking Detmer six times. The loss put the Cougars 0 and 3. They had also lost their first game of the season to No. 1 Florida State (in the Pigskin Classic) and their second to UCLA in Pasadena.

In this third game, at University Park, the Cougars were reeling, trying to find themselves. With Nati Valdez out with a hamstring injury and Micah Matsuzaki hobbled by a swollen bruise in the back of his leg, BYU's offense came to Penn State looking for some weapons to help Detmer. The tight end position, always a key for the Cougars, had not solidified itself. At that position freshman Itula Mili and junior Byron Rex shared time.

The Cougars struggled to keep Penn State in sight at halftime 10-7. The only BYU touchdown came at the end of a 71-yard drive with Detmer hitting Bryce Doman for a 12-yard score. It was a rifle shot to Doman in the corner of the end zone. "You don't see a pass thrown any better than that one," said Paterno.

Opening the second half behind by three points, freshman Jamal Willis fumbled the kickoff and a limping Micah Matsuzaki fumbled a punt on BYU's next attempted possession. Penn State hopped on the opportunity quicker than a starved lion. Within minutes Penn State took control of the game. It was over. And so were Detmer's hopes for a repeat Heisman Trophy. You don't honor players on teams that go 0 and 3.

In the interview room following the game, a reporter from Pennsylvania asked Paterno why Detmer didn't pilfer the Nittany Lion defense like he did in the 1989 Holiday Bowl for the record 576 yards.

Paterno, the gridiron sage, gave an answer which underlined one of the more astonishing aspects of Cougar football, the unsung success of its offense, and put in perspective the remarkable career of Detmer. (Or of any BYU quarterback.)

"Detmer played out there with little help. He didn't have the supporting cast he once had. I didn't see any

114

Alonzo Highsmiths out there in the backfield," said the perceptive Paterno. (Highsmith keyed a Miami Hurricane offensive attack, running and catching passes out of the backfield, leading the Canes to a national championship in 1989.)

Paterno touched on a remarkable anomaly.

When a guy passes for more than 15,000 yards, you'd expect he'd be throwing 90-yard touchdowns on every play of his career to receivers who run the 100 like masterful Jerry Rice of the '49ers, and jump over the goalposts like Superman. Not so in Provo. BYU receivers aren't fast, but what they lack in speed they compensate for by their famed knack at bagging balls. BYU receivers are always known for their hard work, disciplined routes, and sure hands.

In a game of precision passing unmatched in college football, the BYU attack is dependent upon a quarterback triggerman and guys who don't drop footballs. These guys don't drop footballs, and yet, Ty Detmer never completed a pass to a receiver who has made it in the NFL.

BYU's great offense, for all its numbers, all its statistics, its mound of NCAA records, and all-America quarterbacks, has never featured a Highsmith, a Raghib Ismail or a Desmond Howard. Rarely do the Cougars have a rocket, if even a fancy Roman candle.

This isn't to discount the ability of BYU's pass catchers. Quite the contrary, this only highlights the extraordinary accomplishment by the coaches and receiving corps as a whole and the acumen of pass thrower Detmer. This point is—what would have happened if this group could have added speed to its already legendary accomplishments?

The key receivers in the 1990 Heisman year and in the 1989 season leading up to it were Matt Bellini, Chris Smith, Chuck Cutler, Andy Boyce, Jeff Frandsen and a young Micah Matsuzaki.

Cutler set an NCAA record for catching at least one touchdown pass at eight consecutive games. Boyce's 1,241 yards receiving in 1990 is a school record. Bellini ended his career in 1990 as BYU's all-time reception leader with 204 catches for a record 2,635 yards, breaking Phil Odle's all-time receiving record. The NFL promptly ignored him. Cincinnati drafted Chris Smith, a two-time All-America tight end, in the 12th round and later cut him. Cutler, Boyce and Frandsen never pursued NFL careers. Cutler is a financial consultant in Salt Lake City. Boyce works for WordPerfect Corporation. Frandsen pursued a law degree.

There in a nutshell is the group that primarily hauled in the biggest chunk of Detmer's NCAA record 15,000 passing yards.

Amazing? Try astounding!

BYU receivers have made it in the NFL before. Todd Christensen, although a fullback at BYU, earned all-pro honors for the Los Angeles Raiders and at one time was considered the best tight end in the business. Glen Kozlowski earned a pension with the Chicago Bears,

116

and Mark Bellini (brother of Matt) stuck three seasons with the Indianapolis Colts and Phoenix Cardinals.

But Ty Detmer didn't throw to those guys.

It is like Lawrence of Arabia without the Bedouins; Chrysler Corporation without Iacocca; Johnson & Johnson's without one of the Johnsons.

It is, in reality, a part of the legend.

TWELVE

MATT BELLINI:
MR. CLUTCH

The University of Utah found itself struggling to contain BYU's offensive onslaught on November 17, 1990 in Rice Stadium.

That day, the leading candidate for the Heisman Trophy, Ty Detmer, got nearly everything he wanted. Down after down, Detmer pulled the trigger and the Cougar offense jumped forward, marching down the artificial turf until the gun had signaled a 45-22 Cougar win.

In the second half, Detmer caught Utah's defense in zone coverage and he immediately looked for his money man, Matt Bellini, who could curl and come back to passes better than a tax man in April. Detmer's pass traveled just 20 yards. Bellini hauled it in just like he'd done a hundred times before. Bellini turned upfield, and like he'd done a hundred times before, started to slice through a defense.

On this particular play, BYU receiver Brent Nyberg ran interference for Bellini downfield, blocking Ute defenders as Bellini raced for the end zone. Then disaster struck.

Bellini ran right up Nyberg's back. As he stepped on the receiver's leg, a tendon snapped in Bellini's foot—a key stabilizing support that, like a hinge, allows the foot to spring vertically up and down.

Detmer's favorite go-to man was gone. This is a guy who'd converted so many third and longs it was embarrassing. Bellini represented five years of experience in the Cougar offense and accounted for more yardage than any receiver who ever put on the BYU royal blue. During the 1990 season, he'd been at least one-third of the offensive arsenal.

It was a sobering moment.

The Cougars would whip Utah State 45-10 the next week and break into the Top 5 in both wire-service rankings. After that win, BYU would then lose its next five football games, the last two of the 1990 season (Hawaii and Texas A&M), and the first three of the 1991 season (Florida State, UCLA and Penn State). During this period, BYU football became the laughingstock of the national media.

Off the field Matt Bellini wears glasses and rides a scooter to class. He looks like Bobby Darin on his way to see Annette Funicello. On the field he is a volatile and intense football player—a guy who had been booted out of more games than any player during the 1990 season for pushing the game to its physical extremes. Off the field, his battlefield tactics change. He has a definite

120

way with the ladies: it may be his square jaw, his easy laugh, or his eyes (which really do twinkle as if run on Double A batteries). Whatever it is, Matt Bellini has it. Benjamin Franklin called it electricity.

Matt Bellini played as the prototype halfback for BYU's high-tech passing game, which is as sophisticated and complex as any in football. He just might have been the most consistent and versatile player in school history. Certainly, when he hobbled off the field at Rice Stadium in Salt Lake City, he left as a legend—the most prolific pass catcher BYU had ever seen.

Bellini was the master of precision routes. He cut patterns like scissors and sucked up footballs like an industrial-strength vacuum.

Bellini made a living off six-yard passes.

Since his sophomore year, Bellini dropped only two passes which he deemed catchable. His self-imposed grading system was strict: Anything he could touch and get his fingers on was catchable. One of those two "drops" occurred against Washington State, a high ball he tipped to WSU's Alvin Dunn, who returned it 25 yards for a touchdown.

"I should have caught that ball. I catch those nine of 10 times. I didn't play that well," said Bellini.

On that day Bellini caught 10 passes for 121 yards. A routine day at the office.

Against Navy as a junior, Bellini hauled in four touchdown passes. The Middies still wonder how he got inside their blockade.

121

Former coach Tommy Hudspeth brought in a truckload of tough Marines in the mid-'60s to toughen up BYU's football program. One guy on the truck was Phil Odle.

Odle had an uncanny nose for the football. He wasn't very tall, but he was quick as a cat and when he made his cuts, they were instinctive and on the mark. He could outjump any defensive back on the schedule.

Coach LaVell Edwards' best compliment to the career of Matt Bellini is praise of Odle and his record, a mark which stood for decades until Bellini broke it.

"Phil Odle could play with any of them today," said Edwards, "He was like Glen Kozlowski. I don't think any wide receiver could duplicate what he did today against these defenses, which have improved with double man and zones that literally take away the wide receiver from an offense. It is that kind of defense which has opened up routes for a Matt Bellini and makes a tight end like Chris Smith so valuable. Phil was a great receiver."

When Edwards thinks back over Matt Bellini's five-year career, one word comes to mind. Productivity.

"He's a classic example of a guy who produces, whether it's catching or running. Matt played with a lot of pain over the years and we've used him all over the field and he just produces," said Edwards.

Bellini worked as a receiver, runner, punt returner, and flanker, and the Cougars usually sent him in motion as a decoy to force linebackers and the secondary

122

to reveal their coverages and commit early during a play. Because he became such a valuable player, Matt did not, towards the end of his senior year, play against the goal line defense, which limited his chances at scoring touchdowns but also protected him against injury.

"Matt Bellini was a smart player. He's so darn smart he was hardly ever fooled," said Edwards. "A lot of his routes were predicated on reads. He's hardly ever missed."

When Ty Detmer arrived in Provo, it just so happened that Bellini was plugged in and ready, deep in his apprenticeship with BYU's vaunted offense. Like Ty, Bellini would rather fight an entire football team than lose. Bellini was BYU's rendition of the telephone emergency code 911. You dialed this number for third down conversions, big plays, and scores when you needed them badly. Mr. Clutch made the Ty-man look awfully good.

So many times quarterbacks and running backs are judged by their stats and no consideration is given to the supporting cast that helped them get there. Detmer never did an interview where he didn't point out the crucial contribution of linemen, receivers and backs. He never had a better prop to help him onstage than Bellini.

At San Leandro High, Matt Bellini followed in the footsteps of his older brother Mark, an all-conference receiver at BYU. The Indianapolis Colts drafted Mark and he ended his career playing for Phoenix before being put on waivers in 1990.

San Leandro ran the run-and-shoot offense, which hinged on good receivers, especially backs and flankers.

After his junior year Bellini was involved in an accident that appeared to end his athletic career. The day was January 20, 1985. Matt Bellini and some friends had just watched the San Francisco '49ers beat the Miami Dolphins in Super Bowl XIX. On the way home, Bellini lost control of his car and it toppled down a hill.

"My body went out the window," says Bellini. "Only my legs, from about my thighs down, were inside the car. The car slid down the hill pretty fast, and I just put my hand and my arm down and pushed up as hard as I could to keep my head from hitting the pavement. I dragged my hand and arm on the ground like that for about 200 yards. Luckily it was a real cold night and I had a big army jacket on so the ground didn't hurt my forearm. It just tore a big hole in my hand, ripped out my tendons, and ground my knuckles."

In a delicate operation, doctors sewed Matt's right hand back together and carefully reconstructed all the tendons. They put steel pins in all the fingers. Matt didn't have a knuckle in his little finger, so they inserted a plastic one. The back of his left hand looks permanently puffed.

The hand eventually healed, but much of his dexterity was lost forever. Bellini would have pins in his hand for the rest of his life. Yet, despite such injuries, he went on to an outstanding senior year, earning all-Northern California honors as a receiver.

Although recruited by several colleges, including Utah, Bellini chose BYU and the Cougar coaches liked him because of Mark. They both had good football instincts. Matt redshirted his first year at BYU, learning and watching. In a rare feat in Provo, he broke in the starting lineup as a freshman in 1987. That early jump provided a solid foundation to break Phil Odle's 24-year-old school receiving record.

Bellini is never one to mince words. His senior year, the year of Detmer's Heisman, Bellini honestly believed the Cougar offense could move the football on anybody. But it all depended on Detmer. Says Bellini:

"It's the little things he does, like keeping a drive alive, making a play work, coming up with a great move. Those are the things that make all the difference in the world. You can teach a quarterback a lot, but a lot of it is natural born instincts. Our two-minute drill is as good as I've seen in football—as good as anyone's. It's simply the best in football."

It is no secret Bellini doesn't mind mixing bones in a rumble if he wants to prove a point on the football field. Officials booted him out of games at Utah State and San Diego State in 1989 and the opener at UTEP in 1990.

But organized (and refereed) aggression can't be judged on the same level as brawling at a dance or climbing over seats at an opera. At BYU, where many players have served two-year Mormon missions and have been taught to love one another and turn the other cheek, playing football is sometimes a contradiction.

As already implied, football—all the pom-poms, music from the bands, uniforms and X's and O's aside—is really nothing more than an organized fight. Player A is told to knock player B on his butt. It's a very simple game.

Bellini knew this to be true. So did Detmer. Good football players know this is the essence of the gladiator sport they revel in.

While you cannot condone fighting, football players play on the verge of a fight all game long.

If there is one big flaw in BYU's football program, it is the overabundance of passive attitudes by some Mormon players, and the overaggressiveness of some non-Mormon or less active participating Mormons to try to balance it out. The Cougars were accused in the 1980s of being an undisciplined and penalty-plagued football team.

Bellini, a convert to Mormonism, always kept his aggressive side and said, "I just believe in never backing down from anyone and never letting anybody pick on a teammate. Football is legal violence. You aren't going to win many football games being timid."

But what about love, sportsmanship, fair play and the reputation of BYU as a Mormon-sponsored church school—one of the largest private universities in the country? What about its squeaky clean image? Doesn't that present a dichotomy for a football player?

"It is contradictory in some ways," said Bellini. "But football is like a war. It is a battle zone."

Bellini's career ended prematurely that day in Rice Stadium in Salt Lake City. He hobbled through the last two games with Hawaii and Texas A&M, but it was a gesture. The spirit was strong, but the flesh had become weak.

"I'll always remember the biggest thrill I've ever had is a home game in Cougar Stadium," said Bellini. "Walking onto the field, coming down the ramp, hearing the crowd, looking in the stands and playing football. There's nothing to compare with it. This is the greatest place in the country to play college football. It is so beautiful. I look forward to it all year. When I work out in the summer, it is all because of that feeling I know I get in fall."

Career ended, Bellini stowed his armor in his bag for the last time in 1990. He had played with a Heisman quarterback—the dream of every college football receiver. Bellini—the Houdini—walked out the door at Jack Murphy Stadium on December 29, 1990 knowing that the cheers in football stands for the rest of his life would be for other guys. When he returns to Provo he'll be one of those former players looking for tickets, hoping to stand on the sidelines with the team—one of those "used-to-be" guys.

No discussion of Ty Detmer would be complete without airing the story of his "main helping hand" out of the backfield: Matt Bellini. This native of California caught 204 passes at BYU, totaling a staggering 2,635 yards, making him first in BYU's record books. Bellini's record will stand. Maybe not for 24 years like the Odle record he broke, but it will be quite some time before it falls. In the meantime, Matt still gets goose bumps when he hears a crowd welcoming a team, cheering for a big play. It's a music that rings inside his head. And will ring forever, despite the fact that his injury will keep him from ever playing professional ball. But it won't prevent him from being in the stands and following the game he loves. As long as he feels *that* chill, he'll also remember his days in Provo, and footballs thrown his way by Ty Detmer. Matt Bellini owns a part of Detmer's 15,000 yards and nobody can take that away.

THIRTEEN

CHRIS SMITH: STRETCH THOSE DEFENSES

In LaVell Edwards' touted passing offense, a quarterback-triggerman is the key. But the main tools of BYU's passing game—next to good pass protection—are the halfback and tight end. These are the building blocks, the cornerstones, the saber and spear of a vaunted attack that has produced a group of players which the NCAA record book lists as the best passers in college football history.

Jim McMahon, Steve Young, Robbie Bosco and Ty Detmer stand atop the passing heap in the game of amateur football and each one of them piled up acres of yardage, mainly on the backs of tight ends.

McMahon's miracle pass with no time left in the 1980 Holiday Bowl landed in the hands of tight end Clay Brown. Young had an All-American in Gordon Hudson, who holds the NCAA career record for tight ends with 2,484 yards (80-83). Hudson also set the college standard for single-game reception yardage (259) against Utah in 1981, catching passes from Young.

Ty Detmer had the use of a two-time All-American named Chris Smith. In Detmer's remarkable sophomore year, Smith made eight All-America rosters. That made him a consensus pick. Smith caught a team-high total of 60 passes for 1,090 yards during the 1989 season. The next season—the Heisman year—Smith caught 68 passes for 1,156 yards. Only two were for touchdowns. But with Smith at tight end and Matt Bellini in the backfield, defenses were forced into a dilemma. This left wide receiver Andy Boyce loose to catch 79 passes for 1,241 yards and 13 touchdowns.

Smith set an NCAA record for tight ends with his 1,156 yards in 1990.

"Chris is such a big guy and he could jump. He makes himself a real good target, and he has speed," says Detmer of the big Californian. Smith helped bring the Heisman Trophy to Provo in 1990—as much as anyone on the team next to Detmer. Pro scouts listed him as the top tight end prospect much of his senior year, then, as discussed later, they dropped him stone cold at draft time, shattering the likeable, upbeat athlete and his dreams.

"Chris was an important part of the mix," Edwards told reporters before a bowl game. "I'm not sure any of this would be possible without Chris." The Cougars used the tight end to stretch a defense, opening the road for the halfback and wideouts underneath or on the sidelines. Defenses normally cover a tight end with a strong safety, but against BYU, opponents usually send a linebacker to help or cover him instead. "It was no match," says Edwards. Smith ran 4.5 seconds for forty yards and at 6-4, linebackers struggled to keep up with him.

"Defensive backs can't double-cover our wide receiver because they have to be conscious of Chris down the middle of the field. That opens everything up," says Edwards.

A normal Smith-Detmer game connection would be 8 passes for 140 yards. Most of those passes were 10 to 15 yards downfield and came at a time when the defense thought they'd bottled up the Cougar offense.

Along with Ty, Smith found himself swamped by the public and press. Like Ty he waded through his busy interview and speaking schedule, mixing classwork with football practice.

A converted wide receiver, Smith had a lineman's body and a sprinter's speed.

But the story of 6-4, 230-pound Chris Smith goes far beyond the confines of the football field. He appears to be a California beachcomber jock with a sunny grin. Nothing is further from reality.

Chris Smith grew up with seven brothers in an extremely competitive atmosphere. His parents, Robert and Kay, moved from Colorado to California when Chris entered the ninth grade. They settled in a small mountain community, nestled between Pasadena and

Glendale, called La Canada. Robert Smith works for a company that exports cement to Taiwan.

For the Smiths, their seven straight sons have been picture-perfect boys. Oh, they had to be prodded to clean their rooms and got into small spats with each other. But otherwise, they were mail-order-type kids. The Smiths later adopted three daughters.

You get the idea the Smiths are into family.

All through the years, people would watch the Smiths to see what they did, how they did it and why— first, because they were Mormons (perhaps), and second because they had 10 kids.

"I think they [the kids] knew they were being watched and responded to that by trying to be good," said Kay. About Chris she said:

"He's a peacemaker. Chris has always been a very loving and caring person. He never says anything negative about anybody and he is always smiling unless he is sick or hurt."

It is the unbridled compassion of her No. 5 son that will make a mark on Kay Smith all the rest of her life.

The Smith children earned everything from As to Ds in school and ranged from athletic superstars to a handicapped child. Chris is 11 months older than Carlton. Carlton has cerebral palsy and does not have the use of his legs. As they grew up, Chris and Carlton were the perfect example of the cruel paradox nature sometimes plays.

Chris may be the most celebrated athlete in the history of La Canada. Big and strong, he was fast as lightning and helped set a national high school relay record in track. He excelled in basketball, where he was nearly unstoppable. In football he played wide receiver and helped La Canada to the most recognition it ever had in athletics. He ended up with scholarship offers from most schools in the WAC and Pac-10, including Southern Cal, UCLA and Washington.

Carlton was the most seriously orthopedically-handicapped school child the town had ever been involved with. Special arrangements were made for him to use the library and he was given a key to the school elevator.

Chris had muscles. His timing and balance were outstanding. His speed was amazing. His physical agility was truly a wonder, and his potential was nearly without bounds on the athletic field.

Carlton spent his entire day trying to make his body work. It was a struggle just to get across the room.

Chris's picture appeared in the paper with headlines so often one month that his younger brother Mike said, "If I see one more article on Chris, I'll barf." Another article came out that week.

Carlton had 12 different surgeries in his young life. After one operation he was hospitalized for seven weeks, using a skateboard to get around for the remainder of the year. "It was a case of a brother who could do so much and another who could do so little," explains their mother.

And it is a story of Chris's devotion to Carlton, dedicating his youth to being his brother's personal crutch.

All his life big, strong Chris carried his brother from the car to the house. From room to room. Up and down the stairs. Chris lifted Carlton into chairs and onto couches. He pushed his wheelchair. Whenever his brother needed attention, Chris was at his side. When schools had their annual trip to Disneyland at year's end, Chris would leave his friends and carry Carlton onto the rides.

Carlton abhorred the idea of going to high school in a wheelchair, so Chris helped him adapt to the use of a walker. It was a painful and nearly impossible thing to master in his condition.

One day, heading to his algebra class, Carlton decided he would discard his wheelchair and use his walker to go from the hall into his classroom. As he entered the door, the class fell silent. He slowly struggled inside the door and took four or five more steps and stopped. The silence was replaced with a standing ovation as classmates cheered for a full minute.

The teacher, football coach Don Schaffman, had tears in his eyes when he told the class, "That is the most athletic feat I've ever seen in my life."

When Chris would practice on the football field, Carlton would use his walker and go up and down the track. He got stronger and stronger.

Carlton grew and succeeded, developing his upper body into the torso of a power lifter. Nature forced him to. He got to the point where he could benchpress 400 pounds, mostly with his right hand.

When Chris graduated from La Canada, it put Carlton in an awkward position. From grade school through junior high and high school Chris had carried him, pushed him, and helped him everywhere he'd gone. Now what would he do? How would he manage? Somehow, Carlton did.

When Carlton went on his LDS mission, he was physically able to serve just six months instead of two years. On one particular day when his brother was having an especially tough time, Chris called the church authorities. He volunteered to go to his brother's mission and help him as his companion so he could serve the full two years. The church officials respectfully declined.

Carlton attended SUSC, where he met his future wife.

In the Mormon temple where the marriage took place, Chris was there to carry his brother whenever needed. When Carlton got to the marriage altar, he was so nervous he began shaking uncontrollably.

The man performing the marriage asked Chris to kneel at the altar and hold his brother in his arms while vows were exchanged.

Chris has often told Carlton that Carlton's achievement in going to school and getting married is much more impressive than any catch Chris has ever made.

"Of all the things Chris has done in his life, his devotion and compassion for his brother is the thing I'm most proud of," said Kay.

In April 1991, the Cincinnati Bengals drafted Smith in the 11th round—as the 295th player, and the 17th tight end selected.

Draft day humiliated Smith. Two months earlier, scouts had rated him No. 1, not 17th. He attended the Combine Camp in Indianapolis with a couple of minor injuries and ran 5.05 seconds in the forty-yard dash. But Smith maintained that scouts only had to look at his films to know how well he played.

One reason he was ignored may have been that the NFL is moving toward putting four wide receivers in passing situations, eliminating much of the need for a tight end. When a tight end *is* called for, he would need to know how to block as well as receive. BYU's tight ends are trained to catch passes, not block.

A *Sports Illustrated* article hit the stands just hours before the draft and included negative quotes about Smith from a Toledo tight end and NFL talent scout.

The magazine story featured tight end Jerry Evans, who was at the Indianapolis Combine with Smith. Evans said of Smith, "He's effeminate. He can't block."

NFL scout Dave-Te' Thomas, enamored with Evans, added another comment about Smith: "I think Chris will look good in a business suit."

The next week Smith, still stunned, wondered what had happened. He wondered if someone in BYU's athletic department had given negative comments about him. Then he saw the magazine article. His eyes clouded up and he shook his head.

Smith did not make it with Cincinnati that summer. The team had veterans Rodney Holman, Eric Kattus and Jim Riggs.

Chris, a very real part of the legend of Ty Detmer, found a job with the Utah Pioneers of the fledgling PSFL, joining the University of Utah's all-time leading rusher Eddie Johnson as the Pioneers' marquee players. Unfortunately, the PSFL struggled with the realities of any new business. It did not get off the ground in 1992.

Smith does look good in a business suit. Ty liked him best in pads and a helmet. Carlton just likes him period.

137

FOURTEEN

JUST CAN'T SAY NO

One of the great virtues of Ty Detmer, and one of the heaviest millstones hung about his neck, was his inability to turn people away, to just say no. Detmer's availability to the press and autograph seekers is legend. Just to please BYU and the NCAA after his eligibility ended, Detmer flew back and forth from Japan twice in eight days. He crossed the International Dateline going from yesterday into tomorrow four times in one week. That nightmare travel became necessary for him to receive the most prestigious award given by the NCAA. On this one particular week in January 1992, Detmer was also scheduled to play in the Japan Bowl. BYU and the NCAA needed him in Anaheim. He did both.

Detmer's difficulty in saying no took root early in life. One day in elementary school, Ty had an experience with a professional athlete he never forgot. It impacted the way he handled autograph seekers the rest of his life.

That day San Antonio Spur star Larry Keenan, "Dr. K," came to the H.E. Butts Grocery Store to sign autographs. Patiently Ty waited for his turn. Dr. K signed his name for Ty, smiled and made his day, his entire week. Ty never forgot how he felt inside waiting for that big star to give him that little bit of attention. Little things for some are very big to others.

"Ty Detmer has to be the most accessible Heisman Trophy winner in college football history," claimed Mike Burrows of the *Colorado Springs Gazette*. "You could always get an interview with Ty, no matter the size and location of your paper; he always accommodated. Guys with one-third his talent and ability wouldn't make near the effort he did when he didn't have to. How many times do sports writers arrange an interview time or request with an athlete, plan his morning or afternoon around doing the interview, only to be stood up? Happens all the time. But not with Detmer. I've seen hundreds of NFL players who didn't have the composure, patience and class Detmer has and they got paid to play."

Mike Stolz, a sportswriter for the *Iowa City Press Citizen*, fretted over an advance story for the December 30, 1991 Holiday Bowl between No. 7-ranked Iowa and BYU. His problem? Stolz wanted an interview with Heisman winner Ty Detmer. The angle he wanted for his feature story would really take off if he could somehow obtain an interview with Detmer's wife Kim.

Stolz picked up the phone and dialed the sports information office at BYU.

Ralph Zobell answered the phone that day and listened to Stolz' request. Zobell, BYU's sports information director, coordinated media interviews for the three-time All-American quarterback. He explained that Ty Detmer and his wife were both leaving town but he would see what he could do.

Within hours Stolz' phone in Iowa City rang. Kim Detmer was on the line, calling from a pay phone at an airport, available for an interview. The call left Stolz flabbergasted.

So impressed was the Iowa writer, used to protocol in the Big 10 Conference and the likes of Michigan's Bo Schembechler, that he sent Zobell a Christmas card.

Over the years, BYU's Sports Information Department (SID) helped publicize a host of All-Americans in 11 male and eight female sports. BYU's intercollegiate athletic programs include more than 500 athletes.

On the men's side, the 11 sports keep the SID office hopping. "We have 11 sports and the twelfth sport is Ty Detmer," explained Zobell in 1991. An interview board coordinating media requests hung in his office. Detmer had more interviews from 1988 through May 1992 than all other athletes at BYU in all sports combined. (No kidding!)

Office administrator Val Hale and football secretary Shirley Johnson handled a personal appearance

141

calendar for speaking engagements, appearances and autographs. It took two people and got to be a part-time job.

In his four years in Provo, Ty Detmer was easily the most interviewed athlete in BYU history. The year he won the Heisman, it is estimated that more than 700 reporters asked him questions during weekday lunch hours and at other specified times. Another army surrounded him after football games, inside and outside the locker room. His senior year, more than 400 reporters made requests and were granted access to Ty Detmer on school days.

The task of juggling Detmer's interview schedule became so complex that Zobell resorted to scheduling blocks of time twice a week during Ty's final two football seasons, asking sportswriters and broadcasters to call in on a conference call setup that served as many as a dozen at a time.

It became one of the more amazing spectacles the SID office ever encountered.

Then there were the autographs. At times, especially close to Christmas, BYU searched out and found rooms to house boxes of knick-knacks including shirts, footballs, posters, cards and photos for Ty to sign. One day LaVell Edwards arrived at work, and after weaving his way through boxes in the reception area, made it to his inner office, opened the door, and saw stacks of boxes of soon-to-be-autographed material packed on his side chairs, couch and floor. "I've never seen anything like it," said Edwards, stunned.

Ty Detmer dropped into the football office periodically and autographed material. Sometimes he'd block out an hour or two of his time and plow through the mountain of requests. It remained a wonder his hand could still grip a football come practice time.

"I will say this," said Zobell. "He made Christmas for a lot of Cougar fans."

Most often the press teleconference calls were on Tuesdays and Thursdays. One-on-one interviews were held to a minimum by Zobell, scheduled on a very select basis.

Ty would leave class, hoof it to the Smith Fieldhouse's snack and grill near the indoor track, buy a cheeseburger, soda pop and apple, and appear in the SID office between 12:30 and 1 p.m. Rarely did he show up more than 10 minutes late.

Often, the cheeseburger got cold and the pop turned warm as they remained untouched, stacked on top of Ty's textbooks on the floor while he talked on the phone with media from around the country.

The interviewers included the most famous sportswriters and broadcasters in the nation, including Rick Warner, *Associated Press*; Ivan Maisel, *Dallas Times Herald*; Ed Sherman, *Chicago Tribune*; Charlie McCarthy, *New York Post;* Edwin Pope, *Miami Herald,* Dick Connors, *Denver Post,* Furman Bisher, *Atlanta*

Constitution; and even the legendary Jim Murray, the syndicated columnist for the *Los Angeles Times*.

One of the more unusual requests came from a relative of BYU president Rex Lee, who asked for an interview for a story in a medical journal. The guy wanted Ty to answer questions about knee braces.

The interviews came off like clockwork for more than three years. "Ty answered so many questions, many of them repeats, I could almost bet any reporter they couldn't come up with a question he hadn't already heard and answered," said Zobell.

For two straight years, KSL-TV outdoors editor Doug Miller joined Ty in the mountains for the annual deer hunt, a sacred rite of passage for the young Texan.

"Doug Miller paid his dues and we honored the request, after getting the O.K. from Ty," said Zobell. So KSL hauled up a portable microwave transmitter and broadcast deer hunt camp live with Detmer in October of 1990 and 1991.

Zobell fended off all kinds of requests by fans, media and gawkers to join Detmer in deer camp. He finally arranged for reporters to interview Ty while just cleaning his rifle—preparing for the hunt. "After repeating that scene over and over again for interviews, Ty had to have the cleanest deer rifle in Utah. Maybe anywhere," said Zobell.

"I think Ty set the high water mark for all quarterbacks in the future of college football," said Val Hale. "His career is so phenomenal, our fans don't

144

realize what a remarkable thing it is to pass for 15,000 yards. We made such a big deal when Jim McMahon went over the 9,000 mark.

"Likewise Ty set the standard for how to deal with the media and how to handle the crush. There has never, ever been an athlete in college football, I dare say anywhere, who handled the media so expertly and was as congenial and accommodating as Ty. It wasn't just the media but the public's demand on his time. It can literally wear you down. Players get to a point where they refuse and demand not to do appearances and interviews. Some of our great quarterbacks did exactly that. Not Ty. He never did."

In 1990 after one of the two Heisman trophies (each recipient is given two so the school can display one) arrived in Utah, ESPN made an unusual request. The cable sports network wanted to artistically shoot the trophy with the Cougar Stadium in the background to be used in a feature with Sharlene Wells Hawkes, the former Miss Utah and Miss America turned ESPN reporter.

Zobell lugged the trophy to the stadium and a camera crew sat the huge bronze prize at various sites, positioning it with just the right background, moving it around like a prop on a Hollywood set. The trophy went from ground level to the birdseye scoping area atop the stadium television deck. After moving the trophy around like pizza at a frat party, the crew decided to place it on one of the aluminum bleacher seats just below the press box. A stool from the stadium elevator served as an elevated riser to place the award in the perfect position with the stadium and mountains in the background. The 1990 Heisman Trophy (BYU's replica) sat balanced on the stool awaiting the shoot. Everything appeared perfect until someone noticed the TV crew needed an extension cord. Zobell ran to find one.

Zobell returned to the area in the stadium just in time to hear a loud clanging crash. His heart jumped into his throat. When within sight of the shoot scene, Zobell confirmed his worst fear. The bronze monster had fallen on a bleacher, denting the aluminum, but barely marking the corner of the Heisman Trophy base. An amazed film crew member quipped, "Geez, that thing is heavy."

College publicists provide a significant but overlooked service in the coverage of athletics. Behind the scenes, without the glory of newspaper bylines or credit lines during games, they toil long hours and weekends arranging interviews, updating statistics, researching records and answering questions from reporters who often call 24 hours a day at home and office. Publicists are often the first to come to a ball game and the last to leave. They turn off the lights.

The SID job is a thankless chore which has wrecked many a marriage and driven many a publicist to high blood pressure and out of the business entirely.

Many universities allocate thousands of dollars to hype a Heisman candidate or plug an All-American

146

JUST CAN'T SAY NO

athlete with elaborate promotional campaigns that include everything from T-shirts and videos to slick posters and fliers. These are sent by schools to media throughout the country.

BYU's SID office is second to none. It's as responsive as rack-and-pinion steering on a brand-new car. The office is polished, efficient, and driven. BYU remains one of the few schools anywhere where sports jackets and ties rule the roost from 8 a.m. to 5 p.m.

In 1989, when it became apparent that sophomore Ty Detmer was well on his way to one of the most remarkable seasons in college football history, BYU's sports information office hummed into full gear. Somehow, some way, BYU had to get word out that the Texan was for real.

That year Houston's Andre Ware won the Heisman Trophy, but Detmer was eating him alive with a more complete and efficient performance (refer back to Chapter 10). It didn't seem fair. That year Ty led the Cougars to a 10-3 record as BYU broke into the national rankings for the first time since 1985. Something had to give.

With the holidays approaching and Ty passing for more than 4,000 yards, the season wound down and there was little time to drop in a pointer here or a hook there with the media. Then came an idea so ingenious that it took the sporting world by storm and played a significant role in bringing the first Heisman Trophy to the Rocky Mountain area.

Jack McMurray, a volunteer worker for BYU's sports information office, suggested to Val Hale that the school send some Christmas cards to sportswriters across the country and put something in them about Ty Detmer.

Hale initially dismissed the idea, not because it was bad, but because it might not accomplish much. Then the more Hale thought about it, the more he liked it. A light popped on in the Hale house that night.

The criticism Ty Detmer's sophomore season generated among the national media was based on the premise that BYU's schedule was weak. Yet this same schedule included a WAC slate and games with Navy, Washington State, Utah State and Oregon.

Hale decided to do something about the criticism. The perfect stage for action would be the 1989 Holiday Bowl. BYU faced the "Beast of the East" (Joe Paterno's Penn State Nittany Lions). But in Detmer, Penn State (generally considered one of the country's best defensive teams year in and year out) would face the nation's top-rated passer.

"It was a big gamble. We were going to do something to get every sportswriter to tune into that game and watch Ty against a defensive power. It could backfire," said Hale.

Hale began a three-pronged campaign. The first stage involved making a Christmas card in the form of a paper tie. On the paper tie, BYU placed the message "This is one Ty you'll like this Christmas season." Hale needed to order a special die to cut the paper ties when they came off the press.

The gimmick tie opened up and inside was an invitation to tune into the Holiday Bowl on ESPN December 29, 1989 in San Diego's Jack Murphy Stadium.

The second step of the campaign involved another tie. This time Hale aimed the promotional ties at getting Detmer's name in the pre-season football magazines that crop up in July but are written and edited in February. On the front of the paper tie was the slogan "Five Good Reasons the 1990 Heisman Race Should End in a Ty." This tie included quotes from Paterno, who called Detmer's performance in the Holiday Bowl the best he'd seen by a college quarterback. In Paterno's words, "Dan Marino never had that kind of night against us. Detmer is a great one. He smells of confidence. He has a great feel for the field and was not confused by anything we threw at him. We threw a lot of things at Detmer that a lot of good quarterbacks have not handled well over the years and were confused with. He wasn't." Another quote came from Penn State All-America linebacker Andre Collins, who said Ty had him running around like a chicken with its head cut off.

Here's the quote from Vince Dooley, former head coach at the University of Georgia: "I've seen a lot of passers, but this guy—I've never seen one like him. He reads defenses like nobody I've seen at such an early age. I've never seen one go to the second receiver as young as he does. And I've never seen anyone go to the right receiver at the right time as often as he does."

Hale took a plane trip to Dallas, Texas that spring and spread ties around tables at the annual convention of the Football Writers of America. In the ensuing weeks, mentions of the tie and quotes from inside its leaf found their way into newspapers throughout the country. *USA Today*, one of the nation's largest circulation newspapers, ran a feature story on the promotion. Eureka! Hale's idea struck national gold again.

BYU and Detmer got lucky on two promotional campaigns. It was the first major media gamble of his college career. If Detmer had choked against Penn State, the national media would have buried him and all his statistics in an avalanche of criticism and doomed him the next two years. But Ty the playmaker came through like an actor on cue.

Hale enacted the third stage of the tie/Ty campaign during the fall of 1990 when the Cougars played defending national champion Miami in Provo on nationwide television. Using Universal Campus Credit Union to foot the bill, Hale had 10,000 "Official Heisman Ty" paper ties distributed to fans entering the 65,000-seat Cougar Stadium. These ties, fitted with rubber bands so fans could wear them before TV cameras, were seen in living rooms across the USA. "It absolutely blew my mind," said Hale of the national attention drawn by the ties.

"This was a pivotal matchup between Ty and Miami's Craig Erickson, two leading Heisman candidates. BYU faced the defending national champion and No. 1-ranked team in the country. This was it," said Hale.

And, of course, Detmer came through. BYU's offense and defense buckled down and pulled off a 28-21 upset of the mighty Hurricanes. Detmer completed 38 of 54 passes for 406 yards and three touchdowns that night; the 1990 Heisman race had its frontrunner.

Reporters from all over the country ended up wearing that version of the Ty tie. "I saw guys wearing it around the office and on TV sets from Washington to New York," said Hale. In a *Sports Illustrated* article on Detmer the next week, a copy of the tie was included in the coverage.

On December 5, 1990, Detmer won the Heisman by a comfortable margin over Notre Dame's Raghib Ismail. The BYU sports information staff won national honors from the *College Athletic Management Magazine* for the tie campaign.

At the Heisman Trophy ceremonies in New York a month after the award announcement, emcee Andrea Joyce walked out before the celebrities and VIPs in a New York City posh hotel banquet hall. In her hands Ms. Joyce displayed a Ty tie.

The three-pronged tie campaign which lasted more than a year and intrigued every major newspaper, magazine and network television in the USA cost BYU about $1,400.

FIFTEEN

TOPPLING MIAMI: A HERO IS BORN

To win a Heisman Trophy these days a college football player must be more than good. He must also be lucky. And it doesn't hurt if he plays for Notre Dame or Southern California. A Heisman candidate must perform in big games. He needs to be on national television. He must play against competition worthy of Heisman consideration. But most of all he must receive support from two of the most powerful sports news conglomerates in America: The crew of cable TV's ESPN SportsCenter and the staff of *USA Today*, a nationally circulated daily newspaper.

Other than that, it doesn't hurt if Heisman voters like you. During the fall of 1990, Ty Detmer became the first college football player from the Rocky Mountain area to win a Heisman. He had the right setup, a big-time game, and exposure on ESPN and *USA Today*.

In the '80s, Gannett-owned *USA Today* flexed its muscles in the sports world. Complete with exhaustive statistics, rankings, listings, columns, game coverage and graphics, when *USA Today* featured it, America read it. *USA Today* began using a Heisman Watch, a feature appearing Mondays and throughout the fall. It lists the accomplishments of key college players. *USA Today* even ranks Heisman candidates in order of how it perceives the competition is going. Newspapers all over the country began copying the idea. If a player appeared on the Heisman Watch, everyone considered him a candidate.

The second biggest influence in the modern Heisman Trophy race is ESPN, the 24-hour sports cable network. ESPN's SportsCenter broadcast captivates the nation's sports junkies nightly. On weekends ESPN administers a double and triple dose plus halftime updates. It is heaven for sports-minded couch potatoes, a haven in which many Heisman voters faithfully languish. ESPN uses former Indiana football coach Lee Corso and Eastern college sports guru Beano Cook as expert analysts. When they speak, America listens. It also helps to have the most sophisticated in-depth game-video-gathering network in the world. At the touch of a few buttons ESPN can highlight a touchdown in College Station or a fumble in Norman. Not only does the staff of Sports Center *tell* you who is good and bad, they *show* you. Naked is the player they scorn. Glorified is the player they adore.

In 1990, the top Heisman candidates were Craig Erickson of defending national champion and No. 1-ranked Miami and Ty Detmer of Brigham Young. Both

USA Today and ESPN had officially anointed them such. So it must be.

For ESPN, having Detmer as a front-runner was perfect. It just so happened ESPN had the rights to broadcast Miami's season opener at BYU. In the world of network television, show business and Nielsen ratings, this was a real plum. ESPN wasted little time before hyping the game. *USA Today* chimed in. This was a matchup of Heisman candidates, two top-notch quarterbacks from schools that had produced some of the best signal callers in history.

Miami's Quarterback Factory had produced George Mira, Jim Kelly, Bernie Kosar, Vinnie Testaverde, Steve Walsh and Craig Erickson. BYU laid claim to Virgil Carter, Gifford Nielsen, Marc Wilson, Jim McMahon, Steve Young, Robbie Bosco and Ty Detmer.

The hyping of the game began early in August. Even before BYU's opener at Texas-El Paso on September 1, writers, fans and players were talking about Miami-BYU. It would be the biggest football game ever played in the state of Utah, by far. No national champion had ever ventured to Utah. Only the NCAA Final Four Basketball Tournament in Salt Lake City had attracted more media. More than 300 press passes were issued to the nation's media for the September 8 game in Provo. A record crowd of 66,235 would pack Cougar Stadium that night, making it the largest gathering for a sporting event in state history. Only the deer hunt could claim more interest—and that lasts for 11 days.

"It will be a showcase for sure," said BYU coach LaVell Edwards. "More than anything you hope both teams play well, that there aren't a lot of penalties and the country has a real opportunity to see some great football."

Miami coach Dennis Erickson agreed. "It is the biggest game that has ever been played there. It is the first time they've played a No. 1-ranked team. So they're going to be about as ready as a football team can be."

The pregame talk centered on the quarterbacks. It was Detmer versus Erickson. Who was better?

"Ty Detmer is one of the best quarterbacks in the country," said Coach Erickson, no relation to his own quarterback. "He understands their offense very well. He is truly a great player. We hope to just slow him down a bit. Craig is a little bit bigger and very much the same player. He is smart and understands the game. The key is knowing where to go with the football. In that they have very much in common."

Edwards told reporters the entire month of September had him worried. "We face the best quarterbacks in the country. First we've got UTEP's Howard Gasser, now we face Erickson, then we host Washington State and Brad Gossen. We play Oregon's Bill Musgrave, who joined Detmer setting an NCAA record for passing in one game last year. We will face Dan McGwire of San Diego State, who is rated as one of the best in the country."

Edwards said Miami's defense, rated No. 1 the previous season, was the most dominating defensive force he had seen in all his years of coaching. "I've never seen a better defensive line. It may go down as the best in history. I saw the film of Miami against San Diego State last year and that defense sacked McGwire 10 times and knocked him down at least half as many times again—and they never blitzed once."

Every one of those Miami linemen had been drafted the previous April except Russell Maryland. And all pre-season publications had Maryland, an All-America tackle, as a top candidate for the Outland Trophy.

BYU would counter with a bigger but slower offensive line. Protecting Detmer would be tackles Mike Keim (6-8, 285) and Neal Fort (6-5, 295), and guards Bryan May (6-6, 285) and Jim Balmforth (6-4, 280). The center was Robert Stephens (6-3, 275).

Miami mines its talent from Florida's vast prep gold fields. The state produces more major college football players than any state in America. Florida produces football players with speed, agility and flat-out dominating gridiron prowess.

The Hurricane speed had Edwards concerned. BYU could not emulate it in practice. Detmer would have to prepare for Miami playing against a secondary, linebacker corps, and linemen who would appear to be in slow motion compared to Miami. The Hurricanes had a linebacker from Dallas named Jesse Armstead who could outrun any player on BYU's team.

157

"Miami has played a lot of pressure football over the years, and"—speaking of The Big Time—"they have been there," said Edwards.

As America watched the drama unfold, the underdog Cougars caught the attention of the country. Could David slay Goliath? Would Miami repeat as national champions? Is Ty Detmer for real? Detmer and BYU could pass on WAC teams, but could they do it against the Big Boys? How about the Heisman race? Were Detmer and Erickson better than anybody else? The hype before kickoff grew. Sportswriters from all over the country focused attention on Provo.

Miami is not the most popular football team in college football. In the 1987 Fiesta Bowl, Miami players insulted Joe Paterno and Penn State by showing up for a press conference in green army fatigues. Hurricane players are notorious for taunting opponents after big plays. Their celebrations in the end zones after touchdowns led to NCAA legislation banning demeaning behavior by college players.

Miami players were also known for talking trash on and off the field. Reporters could count on Miami football players for good copy. They didn't mind popping off and riding a foe because they could back it up. While this was not Coach Erickson's style and he made moves to curb it, the fact remained. Miami players liked to waggle their tongues.

The 1990 matchup September 8 in Provo was not immune to the traditional public relation foibles of the mighty Hurricanes.

Miami defensive end Shane Curry opened the one-way dialogue the week of the game by telling reporters what he thought of Detmer: "I don't think he (Detmer) is better than Craig or smarter than Steve Walsh. We face a guy like him every day. We plan on hitting him a lot. We want to be in his face a lot."

In an Associated Press wire story that went nationwide the Wednesday before the game, Miami players continued to announce their intentions in Provo.

"We're going to try to see if we can rattle him, see if he's worthy of being a Heisman Trophy candidate," said Maryland, the All-American. Defensive end Anthony Hamlet explained exactly how it would be done: "Get sacks and put pressure on him. Hit him a couple of times from the blind side. Get him a little roughed up there, you know."

Quarterback Erickson was more diplomatic than his teammates on defense: "He's a better golfer than I am. That's about as far as I'll go."

Miami safety Darrell Williams said Detmer was "a long ways from being great." When Coach Erickson heard Williams' quote, he ordered his players to close their mouths. "It just puts gas on the fire. See how you like it when you stand right next to it. I don't think you'll get too many more quotes like that from now on."

159

But junior Miami safety Hurlie Brown said Williams' comment was simply a reflection of the Hurricanes' confidence in themselves. "Everybody knows Ty Detmer's good," said Brown. "But we've been working hard. It's hard for us to believe that we can go into a game like this and have somebody complete 45 passes on us, because we work too hard."

Hamlet concluded, speaking of the Cougars in general, "They're not too quick. They're kind of slow on the line."

Tuesday *The Daily Herald* in Provo hired a freelance writer in Florida to find Williams and ask him if he intended for his quotes to make it to Provo.

"I hope they find out about them," said Williams. "I want them [BYU] to prove how good they are. I don't want them to get by on any kind of reputation. They may be ranked No. 16 now, but they probably won't look like they belong in the Top 60 after Saturday."

The supreme confidence of Miami's players is one of its strengths. This state of mind was best explained by Armstead in a Miami feature article written in August 1990. Armstead compared Miami's team to the cartoon super heroes: "We may be small but we're not afraid of anyone. It's like this...we each have a special power. If someone runs past Batman, the Flash will chase them down. If someone runs over Superman, then Batman will be there with his gadgets. And if we all have a big problem, we all come together."

BYU's players took exception to all the talk.

Offensive tackle Neal Fort said Miami was No. 1 and deserved respect, but no Miami player would be wearing an "S" on his chest and flying around with capes. "They aren't supermen. They went to high school just like everybody else. They are playing college football just like I am," said Fort.

Detmer summed it up. The entire affair was nothing more than the constant battle BYU always faces: proving itself. "It seems BYU is always having to prove it can play with the big boys."

Saturday arrived. The time for talking had ended.

September 8, 1990 was an unusually hot autumn day in Provo. It was too early for leaves to turn their red and golden hue. Even in the late afternoon, the temperature hovered around 90 degrees. Visitors to Cougar Stadium are captivated by the picturesque setting for football in Provo. BYU fans, notorious for arriving late, made a special effort to come early for this game. A snaking train of cars lined Interstate 15 south from Salt Lake City. It was if somebody had dented the earth and everything in Utah with wheels was rolling towards Cougar Stadium on Canyon Road in Provo.

Nationwide, college football fans scheduled their night around the game in Provo. No. 1 Miami against No. 16 BYU. A potential ESPN audience of 56.3 million people could tune in and watch the game if so inclined. That represented 61 percent of the homes with televisions in America. The all-seeing eye of ESPN set up seven cameras and four tape machines in Cougar

161

Stadium. Ron Franklin and Gary Danielson would be the on-air talent for ESPN. Oddsmakers in Las Vegas pegged the Hurricanes a 13 1/2 point favorite over BYU. The game had been hyped to death. Nothing remained but turning on the lights and blowing the whistle.

ABC-TV analyst Bob Griese picked BYU to beat Miami. CNN/*USA Today*'s Danny Sheridan chose Miami not only to win, but also to take the national championship. Noted Sheridan: "BYU has about as much chance of upsetting this team [Miami] as the Vatican Swiss Guards would have of defeating the U.S. Marines. Cute uniforms, no ammunition. You get the picture—no chance of upsetting this Miami team." The *Athlon* newsletter's seven-member "Board of Experts" all picked Miami by margins ranging from 8 to 17.

"The Heisman hype doesn't affect me," said Detmer, who answered questions from more than 50 reporters on conference calls during the week. "If it comes at the end of the season, fine. But all I want is to look back in the end and say I played my best. That is all that matters."

Detmer said BYU had nobody with Miami's speed to practice with during the week, so all the Cougar coaches planned to do was have receivers run crisp routes, mix up some running plays and execute. As Ty said, "We're not afraid of their speed. We know we'll have to make adjustments right off the bat once we get a feel for Miami's speed. We always play to prove we can play with the big guys. In this game, we want to not just play with the big guys, we want to beat them. That is the attitude of our team."

BYU didn't install anything fancy into its offensive package for Miami. But offensive coordinator Roger French and quarterback coach Norm Chow did polish up a one-step dropback for Detmer to speed up his delivery. With Maryland and Armstead on the other side of the line, the longer it took the play to get underway, the more of a chance Detmer would be in danger.

BYU had the advantage of playing UTEP a week earlier. The Cougars ironed out a few problems and had a chance to see their mistakes on film. For Miami, this was the opener. And openers are often a crap shoot. But still BYU didn't have near the raw talent Miami did. The Cougars would send three or four players to the NFL off this team, mostly offensive linemen. Miami had the potential of putting two dozen into professional football. One Miami writer commented BYU would be lucky to have a player make the Hurricane traveling team. In reality this was a race between a Volkswagen and a Ferrari.

Right before the national anthem, a dozen Miami players lined up as if in a chorus line, pointing their fingers in the air with the No. 1 sign. The group turned and pointed to the crowd, then to BYU's players on the south end of the stadium. Their hands stayed high and pointed heavenward as they walked into the Miami locker room for the final break before kickoff. In the pressbox, out-of-town writers went searching in vain for a coffee machine. "How can we stay awake and write tonight without some coffee?" asked Edwin Pope of the *Miami Herald*.

Miami scored first on a 7-yard run by Stephen McGuire and the score stood 7-0 Miami. The Cougars failed to score in the first quarter and turned the ball over. Turning the ball over to a Top 10 team is a fatal mistake. BYU committed five fumbles and suffered an interception that night. By all the rights of football, the Cougars should have been on the slab, embalmed and eternally asleep.

The Hurricanes kept that 7-0 lead after the first quarter. But a subtle plot had surfaced on the field. BYU's defense was holding its own against the much quicker Hurricane players. When Miami speedsters McGuire and Leonard Conley ran wide out of the backfield, BYU linebackers Alema Fitisemanu and Jared Leavitt would force the play out of bounds for little gain. Up front, Rich Kaufusi, Mark Smith and Pete Harston were taking on All-America tackle Mike Sullivan and Luis Cristobal. All three linemen in BYU's 3-4 alignment were playing the game of their lives. Meanwhile inside linebackers Rocky Biegel and Shad Hansen plugged up gaps and continually dragged down Miami's backs, holding runs to short yardage. The biggest mismatch on the field was BYU's secondary facing Miami's Randall Hill, a 4.3 sprinter who came to Provo ranked as the No. 2 kick return man in Miami history. But the Cougar secondary would emerge as a key as the battle edged forward.

As the first half progressed, it was evident Miami's offense wasn't going to push around BYU's defense. Cougar defenders had gotten themselves gassed up emotionally. The Cougar players had read all the quotes in the paper and win or lose, they vowed nothing would come cheap. Miami would get nothing easily. Like the tachometer on a wound-up dragster, BYU's defensive players had buried the needle emotionally.

When Miami failed to increase that first quarter lead and blow the Cougars off the map, the Hurricane offense started pressing and struggling. Erickson continually overthrew receivers who were wide open. On the sidelines his Miami teammates started turning against him, complaining he was killing them.

In the second quarter BYU's offense, sensing the Cougar defensive intensity, kicked into gear. In the first series of the second quarter, Detmer led the Cougars on a 60-yard, seven-play scoring drive that made Detmer look like Houdini. Matt Bellini caught the 14-yard touchdown pass in the corner of the end zone. Detmer nearly took his head off in the celebration on the way back to the sideline. On that scoring play, Miami appeared to have BYU stopped. The defense flushed Detmer from the pocket. At the 14-yard line Ty dodged linebacker Shane Curry. Then he stepped out of a tackle by Russell Maryland and took off, sprinting for the sideline. Both Maryland and Curry had their faces in

165

the turf, their hands empty. At full gait, his heart pumping, Detmer had never taken his eyes off his intended receiver. He knew exactly where all four BYU receivers were. Squaring his shoulders to the line of scrimmage, he lofted a soft feathery-touch pass over the head of cornerback Ryan McNeil into the arms of the dependable Bellini.

"He's one slimy cat," crowed Bellini afterwards. Earl Kauffman tied the score 7-all with a routine point-after kick.

Just five minutes later, Kauffman booted a 32-yard field goal to put the Cougars up 10-7. A national TV audience edged closer to the screen. This was a football game.

The Cougars coughed up a fumble on their next possession and Miami immediately made the most of it on BYU's 43-yard line, pounding the ball to the Cougar two-yard line where McGuire ran in the end zone nearly untouched. Miami, defending its national title, had regained the lead 14-10 with 1:42 left before intermission.

But Detmer and BYU's offense didn't want ESPN breaking at halftime with BYU trailing. Chow ordered BYU's two-minute drill offense. To the amazement of 300 sportswriters in the pressbox, Detmer began ripping Miami apart, throwing seven straight perfect strikes. He made it look so easy the Hurricanes were stunned. BYU's receivers had shaken off early jitters and were working themselves into the seams of Miami's secondary, forcing the quicker Hurricanes to cover every square inch of turf 40 yards from the line of scrimmage. It wasn't something Miami had to do even against Notre Dame and Alabama the previous year. Detmer drove BYU to the Miami two-yard line where he rifled a pass to Andy Boyce while under pressure. Before ESPN faded to a commercial break BYU led No. 1 Miami 17-14 and Cougar Stadium went wild.

In that first half, Miami had blitzed Detmer on one third down play. Detmer kept his eyes on Boyce until the last possible second, then zipped a pass on target for the first down. Two Miami defenders crashed into Detmer. One drove his helmet underneath his chin, splitting it open enough to require stitches. Whenever Detmer was on the sidelines the rest of the game, ESPN cameras kept focusing on him grinning, a big patch taped to his chin. He looked like a Marine, everybody's big brother, mugging from the battlefront. It was a scene from this game which would remain frozen forever: the *'Cane Killer*. And a nation about to enter a war called Desert Storm had a hero. Detmer will carry that scar the rest of his life, a ripple under the tip of his chin. "I'll take six stitches for a good deep sideline pattern anytime," Detmer told reporters after.

At halftime it was as if a power line had been knocked down, spewing bolts in a circle around the Cougar Stadium bowl. You could measure the electricity with a volt meter. One BYU fan suffered a heart attack in the first quarter. An ambulance rushed him to nearby

Utah Valley Regional Medical Center. When it was determined it was only a "mild" attack, he requested and was granted permission to return to the stadium. The Cougars were on top of college football's powerhouse. BYU did it in spite of three fumbles and Miami's interception of Detmer's pass to BYU receiver Brent Nyberg.

Miami had allowed just 270 yards per game the previous year, but swallowed 332 yards from the Cougar offense the first 30 minutes. Executing a game plan that called for throwing underneath routes, Detmer completed passes for 200 yards in the second quarter alone. After the first quarter a writer from *The Palm Beach Post* called his desk back in Florida and reported, "I can't believe it. BYU's slow white guys are open all over the field."

The second half opened with Erickson taking Miami down the field 80 yards, where Conley scored from the seven. The Hurricanes made it look easy and the ecstatic crowd wondered if the emotion spent the first 30 minutes would catch up with BYU, leaving the Cougars flat and dead. Miami led 21-17. But it was all the scoring the No. 1 team would do the rest of the night.

Kauffman capped a Cougar drive by drilling a 29-yard field goal to draw BYU within one at 21-20 with 9:26 remaining in the third quarter. One minute later Miami's Coach Erickson, his team needing insurance points, gambled on fourth-and-one on his own 44-yard line. This was a pivotal play, maybe the biggest of the game. If Miami gained the first down, the 'Canes would score and take control of the game, a contest they were only in because of BYU turnovers. Quarterback Craig Erickson took the snap and handed off to McGuire who headed for BYU's defensive line. McGuire earlier had delivered two scoring runs with little effort. There was little reason to doubt he'd pick up the necessary yardage for Miami.

But BYU's defense had not expended all of its pent-up adrenalin. It would cut Miami no slack. Not this night. Not the rest of the game. If the Cougar defenders never played another down of football in their lives, they knew this game would last forever in their minds and hearts. And, of course, their video libraries. They weren't about to cheat themselves on one fourth-down play.

McGuire never made it past the line of scrimmage as Harston, Kaufusi and Biegel swarmed over him, then buried him in a pile.

BYU took possession at the Miami 43 and in nine plays Detmer rocked the Hurricane defense with another pinpoint pass.

Of the crucial play, *Denver Post* columnist Dick Connor reported: "One freeze frame should be blown up and left on the locker room wall. It will show Miami defenders Kipp Vickers, Shane Curry, Jessie Armstead and Eric Miller all stomach down.

"Meanwhile, seven yards up in the end zone, Mike Salido had the winning touchdown. And standing over

169

the flattened quartet, Detmer was clapping his hands with glee.

"When the play started, Salido was a junior. By the time Detmer ran around, shed one tackler after another, waited for somebody to come open and finally found Salido, he was a senior.

"Detmer pumped, pulled the ball in, ran, pumped again, twisted, had Vickers and Curry knock each other off the play as they collided, then spotted Salido sneaking across the end zone."

BYU went for two points instead of the one-point PAT. Once again Detmer played Houdini, bootlegging around the end and rifling a pass to Boyce as defender Darryl Williams, on his knees, could do nothing but rip up pieces of grass. Williams was not popping off any more that night. BYU led 28-21 and had dominated the overconfident 'Canes.

Miami didn't die easily that night. Twice in the fourth quarter, Erickson, shrugging off his complaining teammates, threw potential touchdown passes. One more BYU hero stepped forward and played his way into glory on national television. Cougar cornerback Ervin Lee, the lightest player on BYU's team, intercepted Erickson in the end zone to kill one drive. Then, in the closing minutes of the game, he tipped away a fourth down pass inside BYU's five-yard line.

When the clock wound down, BYU fans bolted down from the stands, hopping over guard rails, rushing down ramps, flooding the field. It was the most emotional scene by a large crowd in state history. Police guarded the goalposts as students hopped onto each other's shoulders. Others mobbed the football team.

That night BYU had its one chance to sing a chorus of how it deserved respect. That night Ty Detmer had his one and only big stage to show America he was for real. Detmer had to make his move towards the Heisman Trophy in one single night. The playmaker delivered. The team sang like a choir.

Detmer completed 38 of 54 passes for 406 yards and three touchdowns. Nobody had done that on Miami since the famous Boston College game of 1984 when Doug Flutie notched 472, including his famed Hail Mary pass.

"I felt good about my performance," said Detmer afterwards. "I'm not one to say much about what I've done but this was a big win and I can honestly say I didn't throw a pass I didn't feel good about afterwards."

Edwards, who has been at the top, has a national championship trophy in his office, and has won national coach of the year honors in 1984, thought he'd seen it all.

"If someone would have told me we would have six turnovers and beat Miami, I'd have asked them to give him a saliva test," he said.

In the president's reception room half an hour later, coaches Erickson and Edwards met with reporters. Waiting his turn at the microphone, Detmer found a telephone near the lobby door by the restrooms. He phoned home. While Edwards and Erickson explained the night, the game, the plays, Detmer could be heard giggling over the mouthpiece to Sonny.

National reaction from ESPN's September 8, 1990 prime-time jewel was swift and decisive:

Tom Mees, ESPN sports commentator: "They haven't had a night like this in Utah since someone drove in the Golden Spike in Promontory Point."

Edwin Pope, a columnist for the *Miami Herald*: "BYU's 28-21 stunner at Provo, Utah was devoid of the slightest iota of flukishness. It could have been inordinately worse. Miami hasn't been handled so brutally since Tennessee did it, 35-10, in the Sugar Bowl at the end of the 1985 season." Continued Pope: "There is only one Detmer.... Even Miami can't defend against perfectly thrown passes. That's about all Detmer delivered. If he isn't Heisman Trophy stuff, there's not a Mormon in Utah."

Mark Whicker, *Orange County Register*: "Perhaps Miami had talked once too often, or maybe Brigham Young had heard too much. Regardless, the Cougars' 28-21 toppling of the Hurricanes Saturday was not based on charity, chicanery or legerdemain. They won with their hearts. The Cougars beat up Miami's veteran offensive line, tagged the Hurricanes' brash receivers. And they had a quarterback, Ty Detmer, who had fuzz on his face but devilment in his soul."

Ed Sherman, *Chicago Tribune:* "Is it possible to win the Heisman Trophy in September? It is if your name is

Ty Detmer and you rip apart Miami on national television. Fewer games will have more impact on all things important in college football than Brigham Young's 28-21 upset over No. 1 Miami Saturday in front of 66,235 fans at Cougar Stadium.

"While the modest Detmer wouldn't acknowledge it, there's no denying whom the Heisman favorite is now. All the junior quarterback did was complete 38 of 54 passes for 406 yards and three touchdowns. And he did it against last year's top-ranked team."

Dick Connor, *Denver Post*: "Whatever you have ever heard about this splintery (6-0, 170 pounds) latest model of BYU quarterback, forget it. He's better than that.

"This was billed as the early battle for the Heisman, Detmer against Miami's Craig Erickson, two of the nation's top passers on a 90-degree night next to the Wasatch. But it was Erickson who was supposedly hardened to this kind of thing, steeled in national championship games and battles with Notre Dame.

"He was good on a night Detmer ruined the grade curve."

Mike Lopresti, *USA Today*: "The Heisman is his [Detmer's] to lose."

Russ White, *Orlando Sentinel*: "That is the single best performance I've ever seen. This has to be the earliest they've awarded the Heisman Trophy. I gave it to him in my third paragraph."

Ivan Maisel, *Dallas Morning News*: "What was impressive is seeing what Miami threw at BYU and seeing how Detmer created those numbers. That was impressive. People out here are sensitive to recognition they receive, but Detmer had one shot on the national stage and he made the most of it."

The next day Detmer granted Maisel, Beano Cook of "Inside College Sports" (CBS Radio), Gary Binford of the *New York Daily News* and Associated Press college editor Rick Warner the only Sunday interview of his college career. Detmer preferred that Sunday be a day of healing after the wars of Saturday. It concluded a week of pressure, a day of glory, a game in which he probably won the coveted Heisman.

Once again, David slew Goliath.

SIXTEEN

SINGING THE HEISMAN BLUES

When the curtains closed on the 1990 college football season, BYU's 28-21 upset of Miami became just a cherished memory for the Cougars. How do you top beating No. 1 Miami?

The next week BYU clobbered Washington State 50-36. It wasn't easy. Washington jumped on BYU 20-7 after the first quarter of play and lengthened it to 29-7 by halftime.

The newly crowned Goliath killers appeared doomed at the end of the third quarter with Washington still at 29-14 advantage. This team from the Pac-10 was humbling the Cougars in Provo.

But Detmer led BYU back with a 36-point fourth quarter, throwing touchdown passes of 16 yards to Brent Nyberg, 32 to Andy Boyce, a two-point conversion to Chris Smith, and a nine-yard pass to Stacey Corley. Detmer had five touchdown passes for the day, completing 32 of 50 passes for 448 yards with two interceptions.

The next week the Cougars clobbered San Diego State 62-34. Ty had 514 yards passing and BYU had its fourth straight victory.

At this point in the season, Detmer was the Heisman frontrunner. Everything appeared clear sailing.

Then suddenly a new crisis appeared. Ty suffered a deep ligament bruise on his right hand. It became so sore he couldn't grip a football. With the national media continuing to appear during practice sessions all week, Detmer didn't throw a pass. He was at practice, but just fooled around throwing with his left hand. None of the reporters picked up on the injury. (LaVell Edwards put out the word that nobody was to know). Edwards didn't want Saturday's opponent, the University of Oregon, to know Ty was hurt. In the meantime, up in Eugene, the Oregon Ducks were fuming over quotes attributed to BYU tight end Chris Smith saying BYU could score 50 points on the Ducks. By the time the Cougars arrived in Eugene with an injured Detmer, Oregon was primed and ready. Their team featured an outstanding quarterback in Bill Musgrave and Ty's injury wasn't the only problem for the Cougars. Washington and San Diego State had already proved that the Cougar defense was vulnerable to the pass.

September 29, 1990, the undefeated Cougars got a dose of reality. Detmer took his first practice throws of the week in Eugene and the Cougars no sooner walked into Autzen Stadium when Oregon hopped on BYU 25-10, then coasted to a 32-16 victory. The only bright spot for BYU, playing on national television, was a 69-yard pass play from Detmer to Micah Matsuzaki. Matt Bellini caught five passes and moved past Phil Odle as the school's all-time receiver. As the Cougars walked off the field, Oregon's fans taunted Smith for his comments. The Cougars, at 4-1, were back to earth.

Oregon was the first and only loss until Heisman day: the Cougars blitzed Colorado State 52-9, New Mexico 55-31, Air Force 54-7, Wyoming 45-14, Utah 45-22, and Utah State 45-10.

In those games Detmer's interception ratio climbed steadily as the Cougars kept slinging and gunning passes all over the field. "It was kind of wild," said Detmer, who was throwing passes to coverage he normally wouldn't, just to get a big play. After San Diego State, Ty's passing game stats were 442 yards at Oregon, 316 at Colorado State, 464 at New Mexico, 484 at Wyoming, 451 at Utah, 560 at Utah State and 319 at Hawaii.

After the Oregon loss, two Heisman contenders moved to the forefront. They included Notre Dame's Raghib Ismail, a talented receiver and kickoff return specialist, and Virginia quarterback Shawn Moore. Detmer thought Moore was ahead of him in the Heisman race because Moore's passing efficiency was better (fewer interceptions). But Moore injured his finger late in the season and Virginia lost to Georgia Tech. Ty also worried about Ismail. With Notre Dame's great public relations machine behind him and his weekly appearances on national television, Ismail appeared to have momentum. By the end of November the wire polls ranked BYU No. 4 in the nation. Sporting a 10-1 record, BYU had an outside chance at a national title. Not a big one, but a chance just the same. Despite the competition, Ty Detmer was the leading Heisman Trophy candidate from start to finish. In 1989, that super sophomore season, Detmer had finished ninth in Heisman voting. (Ahead of him were eventual winner Andre Ware of Houston; Anthony Thompson, a running back from Indiana; Major Harris, a quarterback from West Virginia; Tony Rice of Notre Dame; and Darian Hagan, an option quarterback from Colorado.)

Ty never felt overconfident that he would win the Heisman, even after the win over Miami. The first time he really thought the Heisman dream would come true was Friday, November 30, the day before the formal announcement in Honolulu. Somebody showed him a *USA Today* article which predicted he would win the Heisman by a comfortable margin. Ty's feet and heart were light that day. It had been a long season.

The man for whom the Heisman Trophy is named was a 150-pound center who loved theater as much as the drama of football.

"No, not many remember John William Heisman, the Shakespearean actor," says Dr. Raymond Earl DeSpain Jr., a researcher at Texas A&M whose Heisman biography sheds light on the legendary football coach.

Heisman was a self-styled intellectual who not only had great passion for theater, but exercised the self-discipline needed to become a shrewd entrepreneur, accomplished writer and brilliant turn-of-the-century attorney.

In fact, Heisman would have practiced law full-time if not for a freak injury he suffered at Madison Square Garden while playing football for the University of Pennsylvania. The Garden's galvanic lighting impaired Heisman's vision, and the team physician advised him to rest his eyes for two years.

Not one to waste time, Heisman began to coach, launching a 36-year career. Only Alonzo Stagg's 55-year career was longer.

"Many of Heisman's accomplishments have been overshadowed by the trophy that immortalizes his name," says the former Texas A&M doctoral student.

Heisman's genius shone early. In 1887, he was named salutatorian at Titusville High School in Pennsylvania and began to pursue law at Brown University. At 144 pounds, he also played on Brown's football team.

Two years later, Heisman transferred to the University of Pennsylvania, where he continued to pursue a law degree and play football. Having beefed up to 156 pounds, he anchored Penn's interior offensive line.

Heisman obtained his degree in 1892 and later that year accepted his first coaching job at Oberlin College.

As a harbinger of things to come, the rookie coach led the Oberlin Yeomen to a perfect 7-0 season that included wins over modern-day powerhouses Ohio State and Michigan.

Heisman went on to become a journeyman coach, making stops at Buchtel, Auburn, Clemson, Georgia Tech, Pennsylvania, and Washington and Jefferson before closing his career with a four-year stay at Rice and an overall record of 185-70-11 (69.5 winning percentage).

Although Heisman made waves wherever he coached, his years at Georgia Tech (1904-19) secured his legend. During those years, he posted a 101-29-6 record that included three consecutive undefeated seasons and a 1917 national championship.

But it was theater and not the opportunity to coach at struggling Georgia Tech that drew Heisman to Atlanta.

Tech President Lyman Hall told Heisman, "The theaters in Atlanta alone draw more people to watch their performances than we have spectators at our home games."

Hall meant to express Tech's need for a quality coach, but Heisman focused on Atlanta's theaters and signed a contract soon thereafter.

John Heisman dabbled in a lot of things. He got involved in real estate and sporting goods and was reportedly a shrewd investor, but obviously his primary love was acting.

180

Heisman typically addressed his players in Macbethean tones, and in his fiery locker room orations coined such phrases as "Better to have died as a small boy than to fumble this football" and "Every man Jack of you remember that in any fight for glory, it's the heart that tells the story." Heisman also proved eloquent with a typewriter. He composed an all-encompassing book entitled *Principles of Football* and regularly wrote football pieces for magazines.

When Heisman wasn't cranking out his own copy, he provided plenty for others to write about. Everyone had a few words for Heisman when his 1916 Georgia Tech team pounded Cumberland 222-0, in the most lopsided game in collegiate football history. But Heisman later explained that he was trying to make a statement to pollsters. "We just wanted to show folks that running up the score on a lesser opponent was no major feat to be accomplished," he said.

And when Heisman spoke, people listened. He not only led perennially losing teams to championships, but also completely revolutionized American football.

Heisman is credited with many of football's multiple movement offensive schemes, including the "Heisman shift," permitted lateral moves before the snap of the ball. He also put into practice the modern-day platoon system and was the first to suggest dividing football games into four quarters.

Heisman the strategist also had a knack for looking at the game from a fan's perspective. He created "yell

181

leaders" and conceived football's first scoreboard, complete with down and yardage indicators, to heighten fan interest.

But few innovations, if any, have advanced football further than the forward pass. Heisman didn't exactly invent the pass or become the first to use it, but according to DeSpain, no one lobbied harder for its legalization.

The forward pass actually evolved from a busted play in a scrimmage between North Carolina and Georgia. Trying to avoid a rush, North Carolina's punter simply threw the ball forward. His startled teammate caught it and proceeded to the end zone.

Unable to see what really happened, the referee signaled a touchdown. But Heisman, there to scout the game, had clearly seen the play and also had the savvy to know that he had seen the future of college football.

On December 1, 1990, there was a mob on the patio of the Princess Kaiulani Hotel in Honolulu. A national television audience keyed in on ceremonies from New York City and Honolulu, as Ty Detmer won the Heisman Trophy.

Sonny and Betty Detmer, brother Koy and sisters Dee and Lori watched the ceremonies on television while in a room under the football stadium in Kingsville, Texas. Sonny's Mission Eagles were playing a state playoff game against San Antonio Madison soon after. Back in San Antonio, Paw Paw and Maw Maw

Detmer watched the screen as C. Peter Lamos of the Downtown Athletic Club uttered the magical words:

"For the 56th time since Jay Berwanger won the award in 1935, it is the special privilege of the Downtown Athletic Club and its membership composed of thousands of men and women, residents throughout these United States, to join me in letting the country know the name of this year's greatest football player—the winner of the 1990 Heisman Award—whose name is Ty Detmer. Ty Detmer of BYU. Ty Detmer!"

Polite applause cropped up in the New York hotel where Lamos and the Heisman network coverage originated. Present at the scene were runner-up Raghib Ismail of Notre Dame, Eric Bieniemy of Colorado, and quarterback Shawn Moore of Virginia. A fourth candidate, Houston quarterback David Klingler, joined the ceremonies via satellite from Japan where his Cougars played Arizona State.

In Honolulu it was bedlam. An entire football team celebrated. A thunderous roar erupted and could be heard down the block on Waikiki Beach. Throngs of Japanese tourists stopped dead in their tracks, wondering what anarchy was causing this strange American animation.

LaVell Edwards grabbed Detmer and gave him a bear hug as teammates cheered and the coaching staff of Roger French, Norm Chow, Lance Reynolds, Dick

183

Felt, Claude Bassett, Tom Ramage, Ken Schmidt, Robbie Bosco and Chris Pella openly wept.

Detmer became the first collegian ever to pass for more than 5,000 yards. To be exact, his 1990 season total of 5,188 established the NCAA standard, erasing a one-year-old mark by Andre Ware of Houston.

That season Detmer set 47 NCAA records.

Euphoria reigned at the headquarters of BYU's nationally-ranked football team that Saturday afternoon. Defensive tackle Rich Kaufusi picked up Ty and threw him into the pool as soon as TV cameras switched back to Heisman Central in New York.

The only thing left that day was a game with WAC rival Hawaii in Aloha Stadium. In many regards, the Rainbow Warriors were the last thing on the minds of BYU's football team members. They'd battled long and hard all season. They'd whipped Miami. They'd gone 10-1, their only blemish a loss to Oregon in Eugene. The press had hounded Ty all year. Most of the defense had played with injuries and at least three players, cornerback Tony Crutchfield and linebackers Rocky Biegel and Shad Hansen, required surgery. Two starters, Matt Bellini and Jared Leavitt, were medical casualties. The Cougars were ranked No. 5 and their beloved captain had just won the Heisman Trophy. For this single moment, this one afternoon, couldn't football wait?

Six hours later Hawaii feasted on its most hated WAC enemy, BYU. The Rainbows, with a Heisman

Trophy winner securely focused in their crosshairs, whipped BYU 59-28. It was the worst conference loss in LaVell Edwards' illustrious career.

It was embarrassing. It wasn't even close. For the University of Hawaii it was simple: How dare BYU come onto their island and celebrate?

It would get worse. For all intents and purposes, BYU's season was over the afternoon Ty received the Heisman. A great weight had been lifted from the Cougars' collective shoulders. You could put a fork in the emotionally-drained Cougars. They were done.

Unfortunately, BYU still had a game to play. In the 1990 Holiday Bowl BYU would face Texas A&M. This was the Aggie team recruited and shaped by Jackie Sherrill before he left town amid NCAA investigations. On that team were a host of Texans who had played on the same all-state teams with Ty Detmer of Southwest High. Ty had nothing to prove. A&M did.

On December 29, 1990, the player who would become college football's most prolific and efficient passer walked onto the field in Jack Murphy Stadium to face his Texas opponents. Within the space of two quarters, Ty Detmer left the game with two separated shoulders. When trainer George Curtis told him he could not play another down, he took his helmet and crashed it against a bench. It bounced and rolled more than 25 feet on the sidelines. For the first and only time in his life Detmer would not finish a football game because of an injury. It was a feeling completely foreign

185

to him. On the Holiday Bowl field, Texas A&M was administering the worst whipping ever to a Cougar football team, 65-14, on national TV. All Detmer could do was bury his head under a towel.

In high school and college, Ty Detmer would start in 72 football games. Rarely had any defense, coaching scheme or player stopped him cold. He'd taken hits, spilled blood, been knocked to the turf, and been smashed and sandwiched until he thought he'd die. But he'd always gotten up. Always he'd made the bell. Until that night. He could do nothing but ache. It was a chilling sensation.

SEVENTEEN

TYSMANIA IN PROVO

It is hard to imagine what a Heisman Trophy can do to a man's life. Only Heisman winners know. Former Texas great Earl Campbell told Ty in New York City the big bronze statue would do more for him than he would ever be able to do for it.

On December 1, 1990 Detmer's life would take a turn and never be the same. Although he stayed basically his old simple self, circumstances of his fame would alter the way he approached routine and mundane aspects of his life forever. Just eating in a restaurant, shopping, or going to a movie would require a strategy. As a public person, his privacy became a guarded and precious treasure.

The Heisman weighed heavy in Provo in 1990.

"What does it mean? I don't know what it means. How can I say what the Heisman means to BYU?" asked athletic director Glen Tuckett. "I don't want to sound maudlin about it, but I know it sure is fun."

Quarterback coach Norm Chow agreed. "I don't know what it means—only that we can take great pride in the fact that finally one of our guys won it. Ty won it. He deserved it."

The week following the December 1 emotion, Chow did, however, find a partial answer to what the Heisman means.

At the Downtown Athletic Club of New York on Wednesday, December 5, Chow left a tux-and-tie intimate dinner with Detmer, his family, and former Heisman winners to find a telephone. Chow phoned a quarterback recruit in Seminole, Oklahoma and said, "Hi. I'm at the Heisman Trophy awards dinner in New York City for Ty Detmer and I thought I'd give you a call."

It was quite a powerful platform to call from and get a sales advantage.

The recruit told Chow a UCLA coach was in his home that very minute. Then the prep quarterback continued to talk at length with Chow anyway.

"I've had that done to me so many times, it felt good to do it to some other coach. It was great," said Chow.

As that banquet for just over 100 select Heisman VIPs continued, Detmer found out a little more clearly what the Heisman meant.

When an orchestra played its first song for a slow dance at the gala, Geri Plunkett, the beautiful wife of Stanford's 1970 Heisman winner Jim Plunkett, jumped up and ran over to grab Ty, dragging him onto the floor to dance. Blushing, it was a pass rush he had not prepared for.

Detmer, in the days following the award, traveled from Honolulu to Ft. Lauderdale to New York to Cincinnati as he appeared for interviews, tapings, and honors. He consistently shared the glory of the award that had come his way.

Speaking of the ghosts of BYU quarterbacks past, Detmer offered:

"They all had great seasons, and a couple of them should have won it. They set the tone here. It would have been a devastating blow to BYU if we hadn't won it this year. Now we finally have it."

The Heisman award has meant instant millionaire status to many of its winners, as well as NFL contracts, bonuses, and hefty financial endorsements for everything from cars and shoes to soft drinks and underwear.

To Detmer, a true champion who still knows how to keep both feet on the ground, it was just another part of the game.

December 1, 1990—Heisman Day—held a special meaning for BYU's own fraternity of record-setting quarterbacks across the country. As Detmer so aptly put it, it was a gang-day of celebration.

Robbie Bosco, Steve Young, Jim McMahon, Marc Wilson, Gifford Nielsen, Gary Sheide, Virgil Carter—it was their resurrection hour.

Under LaVell Edwards, BYU's Quarterback Quorum has stayed pretty close to the Heisman front-runner: tallying BYU's candidates from 1989 on back, Detmer finished ninth in the Heisman balloting in 1989, Bosco third and third, Young second, McMahon fifth and third, Wilson third, Nielsen sixth, and Sheide eighth.

During the 1980s, no other school has had more top-five Heisman finishers than BYU.

Far away from Honolulu on December 1, 1990, none of that was lost on former Cougar Gary Sheide, a resident of Maryland. His nine-year-old daughter saw Detmer on TV during a Heisman report that night.

"Dad, did you win the Heisman when you were at BYU?" asked Terra Sheide.

Sheide paused for a second, looking at Terra, a mixture of emotion and pride building up in his eyes. To his daughter he was the best there ever was, better than Detmer, better than anybody. Rightfully so.

"No, Terra, I didn't win the Heisman. I finished eighth. I played pretty good. That was the highest any BYU quarterback had ever finished. I was OK in my day. But I didn't have a chance in those days, playing way out there."

"But Daddy, weren't you one of the best passers that year?" his daughter asked.

"Yes, I was one of the top passers, right up there at the top."

"But Daddy, why didn't you win the Heisman then?"

Because Ohio State's Archie Griffin did.

In 1973 Sheide was Edward's first prototype finesse quarterback, the subject in a gridiron laboratory experiment by then Cougar offensive coordinator Dewey

Warren. He was installing a revolutionary college football passing attack for rookie head coach Edwards. It would utilize pro-style pass blocking by offensive linemen, convert running backs into receivers, do much more with the tight end, spread receivers all over the field, and deluge the sky with passes.

Today, Dewey's package is simple compared to add-ons introduced and developed by offensive coordinators and quarterback coaches who followed him. That group includes Dwaine Painter, Doug Scovil, Ted Tollner, Mike Holmgren, Roger French, and Norm Chow.

No, none of this is lost on former Cougar quarterbacks, even if their playing time is now history, their only glory relived on VCR tapes and in scrapbook clips.

A physical clone of All-Pro Joe Namath, Gary Sheide transferred to BYU from Contra Costa Junior College in northern California and began confidently flinging footballs in Provo.

In Sheide's two seasons, records started falling and statistics started a meteoric rise like the price of gasoline. BYU received its first bowl invitation (to the Fiesta Bowl) in 1974. Sheide finished eighth in the Heisman voting. A dream took root in Provo.

When C. Peter Lambos of the Downtown Athletic Club in New York City made the announcement December 1, 1990, Gary Sheide was eating lunch with his brother Greg on Gary's 35-foot cabin cruiser docked

191

in Baltimore Harbor—about as far as one could be from Detmer and CBS TV's remote in Honolulu.

"And the winner of the 1990 Heisman Trophy is...Ty Detmer of Brigham Young."

Sheide whooped it up in celebration. He and Greg went nuts. Gary was excited. His eyes lit up like a chandelier.

"I'm glad. He deserved it. He had the best year. I hoped they wouldn't overlook him because he's from BYU," said the former quarterback. "It's about time. It's just about time."

Gifford Nielsen, a 1977 All-American quarterback for the Cougars, was in Seattle on Heisman Day. Nielsen was working as a sportscaster for KHOU-TV in Houston, Texas.

Nielsen was the first BYU quarterback to pass for 3,000 yards in a season. Then Jim McMahon became the first collegian to surpass the 4,000-yard mark in the air. Detmer is now the NCAA single-season passing leader with 5,188 yards.

Nielsen watched the CBS TV Heisman coverage from his hotel room that day while waiting for his broadcast of the Oiler-Seahawk game Sunday.

"It brought tears to my eyes. It really did. I remember back to when we were first getting things going in the program. We didn't have the team to play the caliber of teams BYU is playing now.

"BYU is not just another football team now. It is a national power. And it wasn't back when we were playing."

In 1990, Robbie Bosco joined BYU's staff as a full-time assistant coach. On Heisman day he was in the lobby of the Princess Kaiulani Hotel with the team and Cougar boosters.

When the Detmer announcement came, he raised his fist and lifted his chin with emotion on his face.

Bosco finished third in the Heisman twice and is the only BYU quarterback to ever experience a national title.

"This was a great moment in BYU history," Bosco said. "Ty deserved it. No doubt in my mind. Ty has a little bit of every BYU quarterback in him. Of all the great points of all our games, he has those points in his game. Plus, he is just a great kid. I'm happy for him."

Ty Detmer is a simple young man.

He plays. He just plays to win.

A reporter once asked him what he thinks about when dropping back to pass, surveying secondaries, looking for receivers.

"Drop back and let her fly."

"What happens on some of those interceptions?"

"I throw 'em, they catch 'em."

After a season-ending loss at Hawaii, which dampened some of the Heisman celebration and robbed the team of a chance at a national title, a reporter asked Detmer if, in hindsight, he'd still choose to throw as many long passes on third downs, which cost him four interceptions that Saturday.

"Yes, I would throw the same passes, he said "It was third down, wasn't it?"

Patiently and honestly Ty approaches football and his life. It isn't any big mystery.

There is black and there is white. Detmer doesn't see any gray.

With Ty's super sophomore year and a junior season capped by the Heisman award, Tysmania found permanent root in Provo. Once the team returned from Hawaii, the university staged a big reception. Brigham Young University president Dr. Rex Lee, in a spirited speech, told everyone Ty Detmer had done more for the Mormons than the church's 40,000 full-time missionaries. Lee was using a little hyperbole, of course, but some serious-minded members of the church called the next day and complained about the comparison. It only underscored just how popular Ty Detmer had become as an ambassador for the school.

Within days of the Heisman announcement Ty made appearances on ABC-TV's "Good Morning America." Utah Governor Norm Bangerter declared December 6, 1990 "Ty Detmer Day" and invited Detmer and coach LaVell Edwards up for a reception.

It wasn't that easy to have a Ty Day in Utah. Originally scheduled for that Tuesday, the honor was delayed out of respect for one of Utah's most esteemed educators, former state superintendent Jim Moss, who had died unexpectedly.

Ty arrived on Thursday, December 20, 1990. So did one of the biggest snowstorms in years.

Roads were bad. Edwards and Detmer were chauffeured to Salt Lake City by publicist Val Hale. Hale went to the university motor pool and checked out a four-wheel-drive Blazer. He checked it out early. The normal 40-minute drive took over an hour. "I could have made headline news real easy, 15 minutes worth," says Hale of his cargo and a potential mishap.

Ty presented the governor with a huge poster of himself in a tuxedo, tossing up a football with the trophy nearby. When it came time for Detmer to autograph the poster, he asked Bangerter what he wanted in the inscription. Edwards piped in, "How about 'To the best Governor Utah now has'?"

That day Detmer signed more autographs than Bangerter signed bills in his entire reign in office. "Remember Ty," said the Governor, "No running for governor."

Back at the football office, secretary Shirley Johnson was besieged by autograph requests. People would drive up and dump off boxes of miniature footballs and other junk. It was 23 degrees outside the Smith Fieldhouse, which housed the football offices. Two women got out of a car which they parked illegally and ran to the office, toting a plastic bag full of footballs for Ty to autograph. What the women didn't know was that there were rooms

195

full of identical bags in the Smith Fieldhouse. Earlier in the week Detmer had spent four hours signing footballs.

"Everybody thinks it's a novel idea for a Christmas gift, to have something signed by Ty," said Shirley. "I've got news for them."

EIGHTEEN

FACING THE MUSIC: BETTY AND TY

When a person wins the Heisman Trophy what can he possibly do to top it? In four straight years of Heisman winners from 1988 through 1992, juniors won Heismans. Of these, Ty Detmer was the only one who completed his senior year of eligibility. Barry Sanders, Andre Ware and Desmond Howard all opted for the NFL.

The easy thing for Ty Detmer to have done would have been to turn professional and cast his lot with the NFL, making himself eligible for the April 1991 draft. He could also have tried to play in the Canadian Football League, which ended up signing the Heisman runner-up, Notre Dame's Raghib Ismail, for $18 million the same year.

The supporting cast BYU could offer Detmer in 1991 included just two other starters on offense. They were fullback Peter Tuipulotu and guard Bryan May. There would be no Chris Smith and no Matt Bellini. That duo had ganged up to catch more than 4,000 yards worth of passes.

BYU also scheduled the most difficult slate of games in school history. The Cougars would open against No. 1-ranked Florida State, play UCLA in the Rose Bowl stadium, then travel to University Park, Pennsylvania, and face Penn State, a top 10 team. And that was just for starters. The easy decision for Ty would be to quit.

Detmer never did anything easy.

He had committed to play four years and he would deliver regardless.

"I owed it to my teammates and the fans. They counted on me and if I didn't come back I knew it would be a very bad football team." Because Detmer returned, BYU would not only go on to win a WAC title, but earn approximately $1.7 million in television monies.

No sooner had Detmer won the coveted trophy than the "Hexman" jinx sang its nasty tune. BYU lost to Hawaii and Texas A&M to close the season. Many members of the media who'd adored Detmer in September began questioning if he deserved the award.

In January, 1991 Detmer found himself in a San Antonio hospital, a pin surgically placed in his throwing shoulder. He had suffered two shoulder separations. The first separation occurred at Rice Stadium against Utah (November 17, 1990) and was aggravated in the 1990 season finale, the Holiday Bowl against A&M. The other shoulder, his left, was separated in the first half against the Aggies. It was a third-degree separation. Although he'd already decided he would play out his senior year at BYU years ago, Detmer couldn't quit without a comeback. He didn't want it to end this way.

Detmer missed spring football practice for the first time in his life. He didn't throw a football for six months but he didn't doubt for a minute he would take the field against Florida State.

Things would get worse before they got better.

The first bad news concerned his mother. Doctors had found a lump under Betty's arm in January 1991, just days after Ty suffered his double shoulder separation. The physician diagnosed it as an infection and prescribed antibiotic medication.

In February 1991, the week Ty traveled to Dallas for his first Davey O'Brien award ceremony, his sister, Dee, delivered a stillborn child. His family stayed with Dee, as they should have.

In February Ty was baptized a member of The Church of Jesus Christ of Latter-day Saints, embracing the Mormon faith of his fiancee Kim Herbert. The couple planned to be married in July. The conversion required very little adjustment for Ty's lifestyle. All he had to do was give up that Texas iced tea. He didn't smoke or drink. But it caused a stir in Texas as the family phone began ringing when the news hit wire services, making headlines across the country. That wasn't how Detmer had planned it.

Following that crisis with Dee in February, Betty traveled to San Antonio to stay with Paw Paw Hubert and Maw Maw because of the patriarch's failing health.

That month Paw Paw Detmer died. Although Paw Paw's suffering was over and his battle with cancer ended in peace at last, Ty had lost his No. 1 fan and one of his best friends.

"By the time I caught my breath," says Betty, "It was April and I went to another doctor, who diagnosed my lumps as cancer. I left for MD Anderson Hospital in Houston May 3, for cancer treatment."

Lymph nodes under Betty's arm were involved. Physicians ordered chemotherapy to shrink the growths, the largest measuring five by seven centimeters. By the time doctors performed surgery in August 1991, Betty's body had walled off the cancer, which the treatments had shrunk. Says Betty:

"I never felt any danger. God was looking after me. He knows I have other things I need to do before I go. I had Protestants, Catholics, Jews and all kinds of religions praying for me. I had it covered in all areas. I could feel those prayers working. Whenever I'd start thinking a bad thought, I'd stop and remember 'I can't think a bad thought because there are so many prayers going up right now from so many.' But there were times in the dark of night when everything was quiet, when fear crept into my mind. But it didn't stay."

Her son's No. 1 goals in 1991 were to get on with his life, to get married, and to throw a football again.

"I expected the criticism after the last two games last season," Detmer told reporters. "I knew it would start all over again this year. As long as I'm pleased with myself, with my consistency, that's all that really matters. I have to work within the framework of our system. I didn't do it by myself last year, and I won't do it by myself this year."

The Detmer family had no sooner recovered from Ty's two separated shoulders, the stillborn birth of Dee's baby, finding out about Betty's cancer, flack over Ty's conversion to Mormonism, and the death of Paw Paw, when two more stories hit the national wire.

The first came in the heat of summer, June 1991, when Pro Set (a company which manufactures collectors' cards of NFL players) printed a rookie NFL card set with Ty Detmer. This caused a problem with Ty because, in order for his photo and image to be used by Pro Set, there had to be a contract and money would need to change hands. Since Ty was still a collegian, planning to return for his senior year, the card set posed a legal problem for both Ty and BYU. The university's attorneys issued a cease and desist order for the cards to stop being printed and distributed.

According to Ralph Zobell, the issuance of the cards was a violation of NCAA rules and Detmer could be penalized by having to sit out a game or even become ineligible. Meanwhile hundreds of collectors rushed to buy the card and its value jumped from one dollar to $8, and then $25. Once out of circulation, the value of the

201

card skyrocketed. The story went national. It was a small but very real embarrassment.

Meanwhile, George Curtis, the head trainer at BYU, had begun a sophisticated rehabilitation program for Detmer that winter. It would carry on through spring, summer, and hopefully end in August the night BYU played FSU in Anaheim.

Curtis prohibited Detmer from even attempting to throw a football. Instead he would begin a strict weight-lifting program to develop his upper body. Muscles in his back would be worked on to add stability and power to his delivery with less effort. Curtis ordered Detmer to take a food supplement to help him gain weight. By July Detmer weighed the most he had in his life, 185 pounds.

In the meantime, his courtship continued.

Kim Herbert first met Ty through her younger sister Misty. The Herbert girls lived in a nearby apartment complex and Kim dated Ty's roommate Scott Charlton. There was a small group of friends who would hang around together. Kim and Ty met each other in a clique of sorts—a community project.

"We were very good friends before we ever got serious. I knew her for three years and we told each other everything," Detmer said.

Kim Herbert was a member of the Cougarette drill team at BYU. A petite, brown-haired, spunky coed, she'd thrown a blitz on Ty he had little defense for. Trouble is, she didn't know it. Kim has a lightning smile and was not fully aware she was participating in a quarterback keeper, the biggest play of Ty Detmer's life.

"I kept giving her hints, but she didn't take them," said Ty. "Finally she decided to go out with me and the rest is history."

Ty and Kim fit like a key and lock. Like Ty, Kim loved to hunt and fish. She knew about and accepted a role on the sidelines, patiently waiting as Ty squirmed under the lights and signed autographs.

"She was outgoing. I was very familiar with her. She is supporting, very caring and very patient. She knows what's going on and handles it well," said Ty.

One Saturday before their marriage, trainer George Curtis took Kim and Ty horseback riding. "Well, what do you think?" Ty asked George later in secret.

"Not bad. Not bad at all," answered Curtis.

On Tuesday, July 2, 1991, Ty H. Detmer married Kimberlie Dawn Herbert in Salt Lake City. A reception at the Triad Center drew thousands. A week later the couple honeymooned in Hawaii, where the Western Athletic Conference conducted its annual media meetings in Maui.

Weeks later a new story hit the wires and the level of embarrassment went up a notch. Although the second incident was, in itself, relatively minor, the accompanying national headlines made a big deal of it and sent BYU and Ty scrambling once again.

Shortly after Ty and Kim married, they accepted an invitation by the city of McAllen, Texas to appear in a

Fourth of July celebration and parade. Ty accepted airfare and lodging from the city for the appearance. It worked out well for Ty and Kim. The invitation was a way to get back to Texas for a reception in their honor by the Detmer family.

The acceptance of that ticket and hotel was a violation of NCAA rules. The exact infraction actually split hairs as to its illegality. The NCAA does allow athletes to accept costs of transportation and lodging relative to certain locations from the university in which they play or their home towns. McAllen didn't fall within that requirement, but a newspaper reporter in McAllen wrote a big story that the NCAA was investigating Ty and would make him pay for the perk.

Even though Ty ended up paying for the trip, sports headlines of the incident went all across the country, making it appear as if the young football phenomenon was trying to circumvent the NCAA or cheat at something.

Just weeks before, June 10 at a Kidney Foundation of Utah golf tournament, Ty had won the long drive contest and refused to accept the prize at Oakridge Country Club—because it violated NCAA rules.

"If there is an athlete who has given more to college athletics than Ty Detmer, I've never met him," said Claude Bassett. "It may not be *possible* to give as much as he did to his school, the community, charity, hospital appearances, speaking engagements and church groups. It's like Charles Dickens and the best and worst of

204

times. I'm scared that we may not see another young man like this one. I don't know if we will ever have a day-in and day-out performer like we saw in Detmer."

Betty Detmer is a beautiful woman. She is also a coach's wife. In the world of sports that is not a title. It can be viewed as a prison sentence. A coach's wife is part of things, yet she is not. She is important because she picks up the pieces and bears the brunt of frustration. She endures the tossing and turning after a loss. But she also shares in victories, the excitement of sleepless nights when games are replayed in minds that won't shut down. Nobody understands a coach's wife but a coach's wife.

"She understands *how* to be a coach's wife, and that is very rare," says Bassett.

In Sonny, Betty knew exactly what she married and what kind of life athletics and coaching would provide. She doesn't complain, but there are times she is left alone.

"I always said I wouldn't force athletics on my children, but with Sonny, Ty never had a chance to be anything else. Ty worshipped his father and wanted to be just like him. Ty followed him everywhere he went."

Sonny took up hunting early in his marriage to Betty. It became a release from the pressures and stress of coaching three sports a year. Sonny would come home and head for the woods, sometimes for days at a time.

When Ty and Koy got old enough to go along, they followed.

"I understand," says Betty. "I also know why I don't always go. I do know that if I did, they'd be afraid I'd show them up and shoot something bigger than what they got. I'm content to stay home and let them have their time together. But I will admit it did bother me when Sonny took off to hunt and left me with the kids. I finally came to the realization the hunting did him a lot of good. It provided a big release for him. It certainly was cheaper to have him go hunting than pay for psychological counseling."

Sonny would leave to hunt and tell Betty the place he was going did not have a phone. "If you need me, call the sheriff's office," Sonny would say. Betty would respond, "Well, if something happens, we'll just hold the body until you get back."

Sonny and Betty own 18 head of longhorn cattle. It is their dream to retire on a ranch somewhere and become the "Cattle Barons of South Texas."

The baron idea is one more Sonny Detmer dream, explains Betty.

Ask Sonny Detmer about his wife and he will keep you at attention for a day.

"Betty is just tough, hard-nosed, a great gal, he says. "My wife is a beautiful lady. She's pretty, she's attractive, she's got great features, high cheekbones... she's a doll."

At the July 1991 wedding in Utah, Betty wore a wig to cover her thinning hair, the result of cancer therapy. When the wig wasn't on, she wore a turban. But Betty Detmer, mother of Ty, isn't vain enough to get carried away with herself.

"We were coming home from Ty's wedding and stopped at a filling station," says Sonny. "She had taken her turban off in the truck, and I looked up and saw her walking over to get her soda water and she couldn't care less. She was comfortable. I looked at two guys who were watching and you could see them thinking, 'Gosh, a bald-headed woman.' When you don't spend a lot of time at M.D. Anderson [hospital], it's not something you're used to.

"But Betty isn't vain. She'll put on that turban and look like a living doll. But her attitude is that she doesn't have to disguise anything. This is a battle. She is going to fight it, and she's going to whip it."

Sonny and Betty spent the rest of that year apart: Sonny stayed in Mission coaching; Betty lived in El Campo with her mother so she would have a shorter trip to M.D. Anderson in Houston for chemotherapy and radiation treatments.

Two weeks before BYU met Bobby Bowden's Seminoles in the Disneyland Pigskin Kickoff Classic, Betty underwent lumpectomy surgery (August 8, 1991). Even though chemotherapy had reduced the cancer mass, stress on the whole family continued undiminished.

"Sometimes in the deep, dark recesses of night, it seems like we're having a crisis-of-the-month year," said Betty Detmer. "But I know there's always tomorrow and the sun always comes up the next day."

Florida State defeated BYU 44-28 on August 29, 1991. Although Ty Detmer completed 19 of 32 passes for 229 yards and two touchdowns, the Cougars were no match for the Seminoles. BYU's coaches put only one receiver on the field who had extensive playing time with Ty. His name was Micah Matsuzaki. When Bobby Bowden's staff returned to Florida and watched the game film, sure enough they had kicked BYU all over the field. But videos showed BYU receivers had dropped six passes and tipped another which was intercepted. Detmer should have been 25 of 32. "That touchdown pass [to Erick Hughes], Detmer had to throw across his body to the back of the end zone while running the other way. I've never seen anyone throw that pass before," said Bowden.

The next morning in the *Los Angeles Times*, writer Mike Penner said Ty Detmer's Heisman Trophy was "made of toxic waste" and was a mistake.

BYU and Detmer, especially Detmer, took their lumps.

The next week BYU lost to UCLA 27-23 but botched two scoring opportunities that would have buried the nationally-ranked Bruins. In a showdown of two Texans, Tommy Maddox and Ty Detmer, BYU outgained the Bruins 377 to 263 yards in the air. BYU had the ball 33:08 to UCLA's 26:52, but still lost.

In week three, the Cougars traveled to Penn State, a Top 10 team fresh off a loss at Southern California. The Nittany Lions took a 10-7 halftime lead. On the opening kickoff of the second half, BYU freshman Jamal Willis fumbled. Penn State scored. A few series later Matsuzaki fumbled a punt. Penn State scored. The final was PSU 33, BYU 7. In the first half Detmer drove BYU 70 yards and hit Bryce Doman for a 17-yard touchdown pass. Doman broke his collarbone on the play and was lost for the season. BYU stood 0-3.

"We knew this would be a difficult situation for our football team and for Ty," said LaVell Edwards. "We talked about it. Ty's role this year had to be one of a leader. Our team was young and we had a tough schedule. I felt if we could get by those games without major injuries, we had a chance to be pretty good. In many ways Ty was having his best year. He was leading and settling down his teammates, helping them to win." BYU didn't lose a game the rest of the season.

The next week 4-0 Air Force came to Provo. Detmer completed 20 of 30 passes for 340 yards and two touchdowns. The defense held AFA's vaunted wishbone attack to one first-quarter touchdown and just 280 yards total offense. The victory turned BYU's season around. From that Saturday on, every WAC team chased the Cougars, who won the WAC title with an 8-3-1 record.

The year will also be remembered for a gaffe by an official on the field which ensured Detmer's fame in Provo.

At this point in the season, Detmer had a tendency to chew out his receivers on the field, trying to light a spark, get things straight. It wasn't always pretty, but somebody had to do it. On one particular play Matsuzaki appeared to be pushed out of bounds as a Detmer pass sailed towards the end zone where the receiver was supposed to be. Detmer ripped off his helmet and ran to the official, loudly complaining. It drew an immediate, and deserved, unsportsmanlike conduct penalty from the official.

On the sidelines the official approached Edwards to explain the call. It is customary for officials to inform coaches of why a conduct penalty is called for.

"He said the call was 'bull——,' " said the official, unaware the microphone key on his belt was on. His words were broadcast to 65,899 fans in the stadium.

When the official turned to go back to the field, an entire section of BYU fans chanted, "He was right! He was right! He was right!"

BYU won the WAC championship by tying San Diego State in Jack Murphy Stadium November 16 on national TV. In the first half, Detmer dove for a first down on a quarterback keeper and received a gash above his right eye, another scar he would wear the rest of his life. The Aztecs bombed BYU's defense with a

210

series of 70-plus yard touchdown passes from David Lowery and led the game 35-17. Then a most remarkable comeback occurred. Detmer led the Cougars to 35 points in the final 16 minutes. He completed a career-high 599 yards passing on 31 of 54 attempts. When Edwards ordered in the kicking team in the final seconds of the game, electing to go for a tie, the score ended 52-52. It was the highest scoring tie in NCAA history. Detmer would end the season as the NCAA total offense leader.

In the season finale, BYU defeated Utah in Cougar Stadium 48-17. Detmer's final boxscore read: 18 of 30 passes for 378 yards and five touchdowns. Ty connected with Eric Drage for a 97-yard touchdown, the longest pass play in school history. In the stands that day sat Neil Reed. He was Ty's only representative of the Detmer family and Ty's Texas football past. Reed cried like a baby from beginning to end.

"They used to boot Ty out of his room so I could sleep in his bed when passing through," said Reed. "I wouldn't miss this for anything." Back in Texas, Betty was undergoing treatments and Sonny was coaching Koy against Corpus Christi Miller in the state 5A playoffs.

When Desmond Howard of Michigan won the Heisman in 1991, he did not lead the NCAA in scoring, or receiving, or kickoff returns, or all-purpose running. Yet he did lead the list of ESPN-*USA Today*'s Heisman

Watch candidates. Detmer, the nation's total offense leader, finished fourth.

NINETEEN

BOWL IMPRESSIONS: MVP, MVP, TKO, MVP

It is the dream of every college football player to be in a bowl game. For a coach, it is the culmination of a successful year to be awarded with a bowl game. Bowl games mean success, prestige, headlines.

Few coaches in college football have been invited to more consecutive bowl games than BYU's LaVell Edwards. Since 1979 Edwards has taken his Cougars bowling. The BYU bowl-record in that skein isn't that impressive. But when it comes to bowls, getting there is a victory in itself.

Rare is the career of a player who can play in four bowl games. Impossible is the feat of earning MVP honors in three bowl games. Ty Detmer did just that.

College bowl statistics do not count on official NCAA records. But for the record, nobody threw for more yards in bowl games than Detmer. In four appearances Detmer accumulated 1,175 yards in the air. His 576 against Penn State in Holiday Bowl XII established a college bowl record.

December 29, 1988 in Anaheim Stadium BYU faced Colorado from the Big Eight in Freedom Bowl V. The Buffalos would win the national title the next year, but on that night they had all they could handle from Detmer.

With the Cougars trailing Colorado 14-7 at halftime, redshirt freshman Ty Detmer replaced starter Sean Covey. It would be the last time in his career Detmer would come off the bench for BYU.

Eric Bieniemy rushed for 144 yards on 33 carries to put Colorado in perfect position to deliver the bowl hardware. Detmer tied the game with a scoring strike to Chuck Cutler in the third quarter. Colorado edged ahead 17-14 on a field goal early in the fourth quarter.

With BYU starting from their own four, Detmer drove the Cougars to Colorado's 14-yard line, where Jason Chaffetz, a Colorado native for the Cougars, booted a 31-yard field goal to tie. Three plays later BYU's 6-5 safety Scott Peterson intercepted a pass by freshman Darian Hagan at midfield. A 15-yard penalty put the ball at the Colorado 32. Detmer completed a critical third down pass to Cutler in the middle of the field to set up a 35-yard field goal with 2:33 left. BYU won 20-17. Although Matt Bellini had looked impressive carrying the ball eight times for 77 yards, media in the press box had seen enough of Detmer to vote him MVP. On that night Detmer completed 11 of 19 passes for 129 yards and a touchdown.

Holiday Bowl XII December 29, 1989 in San Diego's Jack Murphy Stadium featured BYU and Penn State. Only two outstanding defensive plays by Joe Paterno's Nittany Lions prevented BYU from an upset. But Detmer's 576 yards passing created a platform for a Heisman Trophy.

BYU trailed 41-26 with just over nine minutes to play in the game when Detmer led the Cougars to two touchdowns, cutting the lead 41-39 with just over two minutes to play.

The Cougars decided to go for two points on their last touchdown. It would tie the game. But on the play, Chris Smith erroneously took his man into the path of linebacker Andre Collins. Detmer fired a pass to a receiver in the vicinity and Collins intercepted it, returning the ball 102 yards for a two-point score for Penn State.

BYU tried an unsuccessful onsides kick. Penn State could not move the ball after Bob Davis hurled himself into the backfield twice, making key tackles. The Lions punted with two minutes to play in the game. From his own 12, Detmer hit Brent Nyberg, Matt Bellini, Chris Smith and Andy Boyce, moving the ball to the Penn State 38 with a minute left to play. Behind 43-39, it appeared BYU had the Lions on the rope. The mighty PSU defense was winded, tired, and frustrated. Detmer was cutting them up and they had no answer. Their pass coverage remained in shambles.

Then Penn State did the only thing they could to stop BYU. Gary Brown penetrated BYU's pass protection, got inside the Cougar backfield as Detmer looked downfield, stripped the ball out of his hand, and raced 53 yards for a touchdown.

With 45 seconds to play, BYU moved the ball from their own 32 to the Penn State 40 in 40 seconds. Time ended as Detmer tried to find an open receiver. Detmer and Blair Thomas earned MVP honors. Penn State won 50-39. The Ty-line: 42 of 59 for 576 yards.

Exactly one year later, December 29, 1991, BYU found itself losing another bowl game in Jack Murphy Stadium. In Holiday Bowl XIII, Texas A&M clobbered BYU 65-14 in the worst whipping ever suffered by a Cougar team.

In this game, Detmer left early in the third quarter. A&M coaches wondered why he was playing at all. With a previous injury to his right shoulder, he reinjured the left shoulder in the first half. He then suffered a separated right shoulder in the second half. The football TKO came from a bone-crunching sack, courtesy of Aggie linebacker William Thomas. The hit and subsequent fall to the turf, separated Detmer's weakened right shoulder. When helped from the field by trainers George Curtis and T.J. Byrne, it marked the first time in his life young Detmer had failed to finish a game.

The Aggies scored 23 points in the second quarter and 21 in the fourth. In the locker room afterwards R.C.

Slocum said he did not run up the score on BYU; he'd seen enough of BYU to know the Aggies needed all they could get. As the game ended, a host of Aggie players laid down on the field and kicked their feet in the air, mimicking Detmer's injury. The Ty-line: 11 of 23 for 120 yards and one touchdown.

In the post-game interview, reporters insistently tried to get Ty to complain that the Aggies had poured it on, particularly targeting him. In true Texas fashion, Ty tried to shrug his shoulders, but had to just grin instead. "If you've got the hammer," he quipped, "USE IT.'" The queries subsided.

On December 30, 1991 BYU faced No. 7-ranked Iowa in Ty Detmer's final game of his college career. In a defensive struggle the game ended up in a 13-13 tie. But a tie was a victory for the unranked Cougars. After going 0-3, they remained undefeated the rest of the way. Detmer was by far the most dominating offensive player in the game, throwing for 350 yards. BYU got inside Iowa's 20 yard-line for three potential touchdowns, only to be turned away by big Hawkeye defensive plays.

Wrote Tom Cushman in the *San Diego Tribune* the next day: "At long last, he's out of here. Ty Detmer is out of our stadium, out of our town, out of NCAA eligibility. The physical damage can be repaired. Without Detmer racing his team over the field like a runaway lawn mower, grass again will grow. Walls and lockers, bashed in by helmets thrown in frustration, can be mended with a clear understanding that Ty is gone off to the pros, perhaps to revive Arena Football, maybe to invent a pinball game, one where the first quarterback to complete a million passes wins."

Trying to figure how much Ty Detmer might earn as a professional football player in the NFL is enticing, but practically impossible. Figuring the exact amount of money Ty helped bring to BYU in his three years as a starter is equally so. One cannot put a price tag on the public relations value Detmer brought to the university.

One could make an educated guess that BYU won three WAC championships and appeared in three Holiday Bowls because of Detmer's contributions. Before he became a starter in 1989, BYU had not been to the Holiday Bowl in four years (since 1984 against Michigan). Traditionally—actually by contract through 1993—the WAC champion receives the host role in the Holiday Bowl. The individual payout for a Holiday Bowl appearance, compared to other bowls BYU may have been invited to (such as the Freedom Bowl or Copper Bowl), is about $500,000 to $700,000. Over the course of three Holiday Bowl appearances in 1989, 1990, and 1991, BYU shared payouts of $800,000, $1 million and $1.3 million, respectively.

It is safe to assume that the 1990 ESPN game between BYU and Miami was chosen for primetime *directly* because of Detmer's Heisman candidacy. In 1990, ESPN paid $600,000 in rights fees to televise that contest. It is also a solid assumption that the

218

Disneyland Pigskin Kickoff Classic chose BYU to play Florida State in 1991 bcause Detmer won the Heisman the previous year. Raycom's package (they nationally syndicated the game) is estimated to be between $200,000 and $400,000.

BYU's 1991 national television appearances included the Penn State game (ABC-TV, $900,000), ESPN national cable at Colorado State and San Diego State ($900,000 each) and the Holiday Bowl against Iowa (also ESPN, $1.3 million).

The net financial income from these television and bowl appearances is difficult to figure. Because BYU is a member of the Western Athletic Conference, its TV and bowl appearance money is divided among the other eight members of the league with a tenth share going to the conference. BYU's share is larger or smaller depending on whether the school is playing a bowl or a conference game. Share size is also influenced by whether BYU is hosting the game or visiting. A rough estimate of BYU's (gross) share money from the 1991 Holiday Bowl game with Iowa is $859,000. Expenses for the official traveling university party and team come out of that amount. Conversely, a rough estimate of gross money BYU receives from a national ESPN broadcast is $180,000 for a home game and $120,000 if the Cougars are the visitors. BYU probably grossed around $100,000 for the non-conference appearance with Penn State in 1991.

If you take the gross payout of the three Holiday Bowls, and add in the gross payouts of the ESPN, ABC-TV, and Raycom broadcasts, all of which may have come to BYU as a direct result of Detmer's drawing power in three years, the amount is $7.8 million. If you figure BYU's cut after WAC shares, it is not difficult to comprehend a $2 million figure from bowl money alone. (Add in the regular television money after WAC shares and one could visualize an additional half-million dollars.)

It should be remembered that BYU would have likely received television and bowl money by virtue of its standing as a college football power without Detmer. But Detmer sweetened the pot considerably.

"There is no doubt that having Ty Detmer on BYU's roster brought the school considerable money. It is impossible to determine how much is tied directly to that fact because of all the formulas and other scheduling factors," said Jeff Hurd, associate commissioner of the WAC.

On February 10, 1992 at Fort Worth, Texas' Fort Worth Club, Ty Detmer received the Davey O'Brien National Quarterback Award. The Davey O'Brien is an honor given annually to the best college quarterback. Ty received it for the second straight year, becoming the first two-time O'Brien Award winner in NCAA history.

That night, Ty paid tribute to his mother Betty, who sat with Sonny in the audience. With his voice breaking,

Ty thanked his mother for supporting him all his life. It was payback time. That moment also revealed the most emotion young Ty had ever displayed in front of a microphone. There is a standing joke in the Detmer household that anytime anything is written in newspapers and magazines the articles always center on Sonny and Ty. As Betty said once, "You know, Ty, it must have been nice to have had a miracle birth and have been born without a mother. I was the one who washed your uniforms, carried you around, got you to practices and made sure you were where you were supposed to be." Ty's recognition of Betty's role in his success made the Davey O'Brien award doubly satisfying.

"That was a special moment," said Betty. "I guess he was getting me back."

In late February 1992, just months before the NFL Draft, Chicago Bear head coach Mike Ditka came to Mission, Texas to speak at a Fellowship of Christian Athletes banquet.

Despite the instruction of her children and Sonny not to get involved in football talk, Betty couldn't resist confronting the head coach of the Bears.

"I hope you'll consider my son Ty Detmer in the upcoming draft, Coach Ditka," said Betty.

"Well, ma'am, he sure shows a lot of guts out there," said Ditka.

"And he's not too small, you know," added Betty.

"Yeah, he's got character, too. I like character. In fact, I should have said more about that in my speech," said Ditka.

Betty later told Ty about the conversation with the Bear Coach.

"Mom, you didn't, did you?" asked Ty.

Said Betty: "I did."

TWENTY

DIABLO TEJANO

In 1988 the Quarterback Factory in Provo cried out for a major overhaul. Who would have guessed the Mr. Goodwrench who fixed it would be a skinny Texan who looked like Gumby but threw like Johnny Unitas? Since few saw the vision, Ty had to show them.

Like the Alamo freedom-fighters Crockett and Bowie became in their day, Detmer became a college football hero in his. In Mexican folklore Crockett and Bowie were labeled "Diablos Tejanos" or the Devil Texans. They roused fear in their enemies and respect from their peers. In the arena of sports, Ty Detmer dominated in high school. He dominated again in college. He lived a dream, a legendary dream. To those who watched him, Ty Detmer became a Diablo Tejano incarnate.

As Ty himself said: "My career at BYU was everything I hoped it would be. I came into a winning program where some outstanding quarterbacks had played great football. All I wanted was a chance to show what I could do. I felt it a privilege to follow them. I had great teammates to play with. Without them, none of these things would have been possible. I had great coaches and a passing offensive scheme that fit me perfectly. I couldn't have asked for more. The Heisman? It belongs as much to those other quarterbacks as it does to me. They paved the way and opened the door."

Quarterback coach Norm Chow, once a scapegoat for unhappy BYU fans during the dearth years of 1986, 1987 and 1988, surveyed the scene on Detmer's last practice session in Provo in 1991.

Standing on the cold turf north of the Smith Fieldhouse, Chow turned to LaVell Edwards and said "You know coach, this is the last time he's going to be on this field preparing for a game." LaVell looked at Chow. He felt it too. An eerie feeling crept between the two, mixing with the cold December air.

Since Detmer had manned the trigger, BYU had won three consecutive WAC titles, earned three All-America citations, and brought home the first Heisman sports fans from the Rocky Mountain area had ever seen. BYU had won 29, lost nine and tied twice with Detmer at the helm. The Cougars, never a great bowl team, had gone 1-1-1 in one Freedom and two Holiday bowls. As previously discussed, the university had likely realized more than a million dollars in TV revenue and appearance money because of their bedeviling Texan.

"Now we've got to go back to coaching," Chow told Edwards. "For the past three years we've just been directing traffic for Ty."

224

Within months of the 1991 season Chow's name came up in connection with openings at the University of Colorado, University of Pittsburgh, the San Francisco '49ers and the Super Bowl champion Washington Redskins. It is amazing how a goat can turn into a golden retriever. Says Chow of his golden goose:

"I will always give Ty credit. The kid just flat-out plays. He's a winner and a fierce competitor. I wouldn't hesitate in any game to ask his opinion of how to attack an opposing defense. After all, he was on the battlefront. He made good decisions. He knows the game of football. He had great training. We were lucky to have him. Ty was a coach on the field. His teammates respected him and he had the ability to lift them up. His enthusiasm on the field was catching. He had the ability to make those around him play better. What more could you want in a quarterback?"

In Detmer's final appearance in Cougar Stadium November 23, 1991, Ty put on a show as the Cougars whipped the Utes 48-17. "It was for the WAC title and we were fired up because all we'd heard all season long was how great they were. But in the end, it was still just Utah," said Detmer. He completed 18 of 29 passes for 378 yards and five touchdowns.

Twice that day Detmer pulled off seemingly impossible plays. Both times Utah defenders had him within their grasp. He was actually fumbling the ball on one play, yet regained the bobbled ball, stepped out of a sack, and threw 20 yards downfield to Peter Tuipulotu.

On the other play Detmer was actually falling down with a defender on his leg when he threw a completion to Jamal Willis.

BYU fans feasted. Their cup ran over. They couldn't have had a Detmer finale choreographed any better. For these fans, it couldn't have come against a more suited foe than Utah. On his next-to-last pass, a catch by Micah Matsuzaki, Ty became the first collegian to go over 15,000 yards.

Just after the end of the third quarter, backup quarterback John Walsh trotted onto the field. Detmer headed for the sidelines for the last time in a Cougar uniform. The crowd rose to its feet. A thunderous ovation echoed around the stadium. Neil Reed sat and sobbed. It was music inside his head.

After the game, BYU administrators began their annual ritual of handing out 'Y' blankets to seniors. Detmer got his last. Most of the crowd of 66,003 stayed for that moment.

Again came the standing ovation. Detmer raised his hand. After passing for 8.5 miles, he wasn't too tired for the gesture. Nearby his teammates blinked back tears. Big linemen, receivers and backs choked back dry lumps in their throats. They'd started 0-3 but won eight straight. They were WAC champs. Their team captain was taking his final bow.

"Ty has the ability to literally lift the entire offense to a different level. When he came on the field you felt it," said receiver Chuck Cutler (1989). "It made a big difference knowing all you had to do is get open and run your route and he'd make the play," said Andy Boyce (1990). "We all had a feeling that he was just going to get the job done, save the day, just win," said Chris Smith (1990). "One thing about playing with Ty, you blocked harder. You knew that extra second could make a difference because if you did your job, you knew it could result in a big, big play," said center Bob Stephens (1990). "Ty is just the greatest. Period. He is the best," said Matt Bellini (1990). "Losing him is going to be a hard one to swallow," said Chow. "He's so good, you can't even describe it."

Many have tried.

Says Tim funk, receivers coach, Southwest High, 1984-1987, U.S. Olympian (team handball goalie), 1984:

Talk is cheap around Ty Detmer. They said he was too small? Tell that to his numbers and his records. I see him being the best quarterback to ever play the game in my lifetime. He's a Joe Montana. If he is on the right NFL team he will continue to put up those same numbers against anybody. He did it against the best in high school, he did it against the best in college, and he did it with young, inexperienced people around him. Imagine what he could do with world class athletes around him.

"Ty Detmer's career is overwhelming. I look at Ty not in the sense of just a football player, but his consistency as a person on campus at Southwest was remarkable. He did not have winners around him. He was a winner who stuck to his guns. Younger kids would go party and be drawn off course, but Ty never was. They looked up to him as the leader, the winner. He was the heart of the basketball team, the football team and the baseball team. Everybody we played wanted to beat us because we had Ty Detmer. Yet he was cool under fire. Nothing ever went to his head, not his records, his honors, nothing. He always remembered his teammates and packed them along with him under the bright lights. I wish there were more young men like him. He honors his word; he was raised by good people. If the world had more Ty Detmers, we wouldn't have very many problems. He is a credit to BYU football and the state of Texas. We are glad he claims Texas as home.

Mike Harris, head basketball coach, Southwest High (1982-1989), says of Ty:

There are certain athletes in the world who can inspire people to follow them anywhere. Ty Detmer was that kind of player. He took a beating on the basketball court. Opponents were after him, officials were after him and he got it from the crowd because he was Ty Detmer. But he conquered it all and performed. He is tough. Ty is a complete athlete. In basketball he was deceptively quick. People would look at him and think there wasn't much there. But he'd play with his fire stoked 100 percent. He had incredible, long arms and could steal a pass or a dribble although three feet away from an opponent. He was an intense competitor and one of the hardest workers you would ever see. He led by example and chewed people's butts off when it was called for.

He could drive through people like Danny Ainge did against Notre Dame. He did it all the time. He hit off balanced shots. We played the toughest teams in Texas, in the higher 5A division. Ty never backed down from anybody. In football I've seen receivers [at Southwest] tip a ball to a defender who thought he had an interception and clear sailing for a touchdown but Ty would come clear across the field and knock him down. He was a consummate competitor who pulled out everything he had to win. In baseball he was an All-American, playing third base, centerfield or pitcher. Opponents would look to see where he was playing—then try and hit away from him. That is Ty Detmer.

Roger French, offensive coordinator at BYU, agrees:

I said after his sophomore year he reminded me of one of the all-time great quarterbacks. I didn't want to say what that comparison was until after his career was over. He reminds me of Johnny Unitas. He looks like him, plays like him and does everything nearly the same. He's a slow, easygoing guy who is never rushed into making poor decisions on the football field. Detmer and Unitas have the same traits. Ty is a winner. He plays football to win. One thing I will always remember about Ty is the Texas A&M bowl game and the licking he took physically. It wasn't his fault. I will always feel responsible. Ty did everything necessary to show what a Heisman winner could do that night, but we didn't give him the protection. We had some breakdowns and he took the lumps on the field and in the press. He'd prepared himself and came ready to play against a great team and we let him down by not giving him the support and protection he needed. It will stay with me forever.

He's just a whale of a young man. There isn't anybody who wouldn't want him for a son. You won't find another young man like him. He has all the charisma in the world, yet he doesn't exploit it. He's honest and humble. His teammates always knew he came to give everything he had on the field and he did it for them, not himself. He expected perfection from himself and demanded it of people around him. Because he was so hard on himself, he could extend his expectations to others and that made everyone else that much better. That is a rare trait. His team loved him for it. I can't say enough about Ty Detmer. There are not words to describe him as a person and player.

Says Neil Reed, multi-sport coach, mentor and family friend:

Ty is a winner. Just a winner. He's not macho. He is a winner. On third base, he had the same body lean as Brooks Robinson. In basketball he had the hands and vision of a Larry Bird or Magic Johnson. He could have been "Mr. Basketball" in Indiana. I know it sounds crazy, but he is that good. He could play in the Masters at Augusta someday if he put his mind to it. That is the kind of athlete Ty is. Even in grade school I could see it in him. If Ty isn't a great

NFL quarterback, then that's the reason I don't watch the pro game anymore. If Ty doesn't make it in the NFL, it would tell more about the quality of the people coaching in the NFL than it does about Ty Detmer.

Ty has tremendous hand-eye coordination. The great ones have it. He's one of the best athletes I've ever seen in baseball, basketball or football. Ty is like his dad Sonny. One was an All-American as a receiver, the other an All-American as a quarterback. I just want him to get what his daddy didn't get—a crack at the big time. I've told Ty this and I will say it until the day I die: Ty is not as good as Sonny. Sonny was the best amateur center fielder to ever play in Cincinnati and could have played in the majors. He was one of the best line-drive hitters I have ever seen; he was a great basketball player and superb receiver. Sonny never realized his dream. In part Ty has. I hope he gets his dream to make it in the NFL.

LaVell Edwards, head coach at BYU, says:

I'll say the same thing about Ty I said about Jim McMahon when he left college. He'll lead someone to the Super Bowl. Ty will be an outstanding NFL quarterback at some point. He'll go somewhere and wind up playing. Whoever is starting will miss a game and never get his job back. That's how I see it happening.

Finally, a little prophecy from Jim Van Valkenburg, NCAA statistician:

You ask me if Ty Detmer's 15,000 yards career passing mark will be surpassed and I've been around too long to say it never will. But if you ask when I bet it will be passed, I would say it will be a long, long, long time. What Detmer did overall was fantastic. What he did in just one of his seasons was amazing.

Ty Detmer's ancestors came to Texas to conquer a new frontier. They were in the front lines of historic battles including the War of 1812, the Battle of San Jacinto and the Alamo. They fought alongside Davy Crockett, Jim Bowie and Sam Houston. They were not seafaring men, but ranchers and farmers, people who had a great respect for the soil. They didn't turn their backs on adventure, they eagerly embarked on the challenges of the unknown, whether fighting the Spanish, the Mexicans or Comanches. In short, Ty Detmer's ancestors were players caught up in life. They sought to win, whether in the daily struggles with the demands of the land or in physical battles for peace and freedom. That blood flows in the veins of Ty Detmer. It is the pulse of a stubborn clan of adventurers who refused to let the nakedness of open prairie or the echo of their footsteps in the trackless woods scare them away from treasures on the horizon—a Diablo Tejano.

It is little wonder that Ty Detmer succeeded at Texas football as a high school phenomenon. He fulfilled that promise by dominating during his college career.

Ty Detmer is a young man after the treasures on his horizon. In his achievements one can see a remarkable portrait of amateur athletics at its highest, in fact, its most legendary stature.

Davey O'Brien
National Quarterback Award

1991 — Ty Detmer, Brigham Young
1990 — Ty Detmer, Brigham Young
1989 — Andre Ware, Houston
1988 — Troy Aikman, UCLA
1987 — Don McPherson, Syracuse
1986 — Vinny Testaverde, Miami
1985 — Chuck Long, Iowa
1984 — Doug Flutie, Boston College
1983 — Steve Young, Brigham Young
1982 — Todd Blackledge, Penn State
1981 — Jim McMahon, Brigham Young
1980 — Mike Singletary, Baylor
1979 — Mike Singletary, Baylor
1978 — Billy Sims, Oklahoma
1977 — Earl Campbell, Texas

The winners of the Davey O'Brien National Quarterback Award. Before 1981, the O'Brien Award went to the top college player in the Southwest.

Top 10 High School Passers Through 1986

1. 8,804 Ron Cuccia (Los Angeles Wilson, Calif.) 1975-77
2. 8,533 Chris Meidt (Minnesota, MN), 1984-87
3. 8,326 John White (Metairie Park Country Day, La.) 1982-84
4. 8,128 Jeff George (Indianapolis, Warren, Ind.) 1983-85
5. 8,005 Ty Detmer, (San Antonio, Southwest, Tx.) 1983-86
6. 7,768 Sol Graves (Monroe, Ouachita Christian, La) 1983-85
7. 7,633 Pat Haden (La Puente Bishop Amat, Calif.) 1968-70
8. 6,913 Jim Plum (LaMesa Helix, Ca), 1979-81
9. 6,726 Joe Ferguson (Shreveport Woodlawn, La) 1966-68
10. 6,559 Dan McGwire (Claremont, Ca), 1983-85

TY DETMER
BRIGHAM YOUNG UNIVERSITY
1991 Honors

Team Captain
Davey O'Brien Trophy Winner
Third in the Heisman Trophy race
First team All-America, Kodak (Coaches)
First team All-America, Football Writers
First team All-America, *Associated Press*
First team All-America, *United Press*
        International
First team All-America, The Sporting News
First team All-America, College & Pro Football
        Newsweekly
Third team All-America, *Football News*
UPI Back of the Year
Western Athletic Conference Offensive Player of
        the Year
First team All-WAC
WAC Offensive Player of the Week (Oct. 31)
Co-WAC Offensive Player of the Week (Nov. 16)
Sports Illustrated Offensive Player of the Week
        (Nov. 16)
Toyota Leadership Award (San Diego State)
AT & T Long Distance Award (Utah)
Japan Bowl
NCAA Top Six Award

TY DETMER
BRIGHAM YOUNG UNIVERSITY
1990 Honors

Team Captain
Heisman Trophy Winner
Maxwell Trophy Winner
Davey O'Brien Award
The Victor Award, City of Hope College Athlete of
    the Year
First team All-America, *Associated Press*
First team All-America, UPI
First team All-America, Football Writers
First team All-America, Walter Camp
First team All-America, *Football News*
First team All-America, *The Sporting News*
UPI Player of the Year
CBS Player of the Year
Football News Player of the Year
First team All-America, Scripps Howard
Scripps Howard Player of the Year
Western Athletic Conference Player of the Year
·First-team All-WAC, unanimous
WAC Offensive Player of the Week (Miami)
CNN Player of the Week (Miami)
Football News Player of the Week (Miami)
Athlon Player of the Week (Miami)
WAC Offensive Player of the Week (San Diego St.)
Chevrolet Player of the Game (San Diego St.)
CBS Toyota Leadership Award (San Diego St.)
WAC Offensive Player of the Week (Air Force)
Amateur Athlete of the Year by U.S. Sports
        Academy (Alabama)
Amateur Athlete of September by U.S. Sports
        Academy (Alabama)
Athlete of the Month for September, *Deseret News*

TY DETMER
BRIGHAM YOUNG UNIVERSITY
1989 Honors

Team Captain
First team All-WAC, Coaches
First team All-WAC, Media
Honorable mention All-America UPI
Honorable mention All-America *The Sporting News*
CNN Player of the Week San Diego State
WAC Offensive Player of the Week UTEP
Chevrolet Player of the Game Air Force

Ty Detmer—59 NCAA records broken, 3 tied
12/5/91

Total Offense (27)
1. Yards, 2 yrs., 9,455—old 8,085, Jim McMahon, BYU, 1980-81.
2. Yards, 3 yrs., 10,644—old 9,640, Jim McMahon, BYU, 1978, 80-81.
3. Yards. by a soph., 4,433—old 4,299 Scott Mitchell, Utah, 1988.
4. Highest average, career, 8.18—old 7.49 Steve Young, BYU, 1981-83.
5. Games gain 300 yds., season, 12—old 11 Jim McMahon, BYU, 1980.
6. Games gain 300 yds., career, 33—old 18 Steve Young, BYU, 1981-83.
7. Consec. games 300 yds., season, 12—old 11 Jim McMahon, BYU, 1980.
8. Consec.games 300 yds., career, 19—old 12 Jim McMahon, BYU, 78-81.
9. Games 400 yds., career, 13—old 9 Jim McMahon, BYU, 78-81.
10. Consec.games 400 yds., season, 5—old 4, Jim McMahon, BYU, 1980.
11. Consec. games 400 yds., career, 5—old 4, Jim McMahon, BYU, 1980.
12. TD responsible, 3 yrs., 96—old 93, Jim McMahon, BYU, 1978, 80-81.
13. TD respons., 4 yrs., 135—old 94, Jim McMahon, BYU, 1977-78, 80-81.
14. TD respons., 3 yrs., 2.82—old 2.81, Jim McMahon, BYU, 1978, 80-81.
15. Points respons., 3 yrs., 582—old 562, Jim McMahon, BYU, 78-81.
16. Points respons. career, 826—old 562, Jim McMahon, BYU, 77-81.
17. Points respons./game, 3 yrs., 17.1—old 17.0, Jim McMahon, 78-81.

18. High avg./play 8.92, season—old 8.57, Jim McMahon, BYU, 1980.
19. Yards, career, 15,031—old 11,317, Doug Flutie, Boston College.
20. Yards vs. one opponent(SDSU) 1,483—old 1,445, Doug Flutie, BC-Penn St.
21. Yards/game vs. one opponent (SDSU) 370.8—old 361.3, Doug Flutie, Boston College.
22. Seasons gaining 3,000 yards, 3—old 2, by many players.
23. Plays, 3 yrs., 1,548—old 1,503, Gene Swick, Toledo, 1973-75.
24. Plays, 4 yrs., 1,795—old 1,722 Todd Santos, SDSU, 1984-87.
25. TDs respons./game, career, 2.93—old 2.56, Johnny Bright, Drake.
26. Points respon./game, career, 17.9—old 15.4, Johnny Bright, Drake.
27. Yards/game, career, 319.4—old 309.1, Mike Perez, San Jose St., 1986-87.

Total offense tied (1)
1. Seasons gaining 2,500 yards—3 by six others.

Passing (32)
1. Comp./game 2 yrs., 26.1—old 25.3 , Jim McMahon, BYU 80-81.
2. Yards, season, 5,188—old 4,699, Andre Ware, Houston, 1989.
3. Yards, 2 yrs., 9,748—old 8,148, Robbie Bosco, BYU, 1984-85.
4. Yards, 3 yrs., 11,000—old 9,433 , Jim McMahon, BYU, 1978-81.
5. Yards/game, 2 yrs.,406.2—old 369.4 , Jim McMahon, BYU, 1980-81.
6. Yards/game,3 yrs.,323.5—old 303.78 , Andre Ware, Houston, 87-89.
7. Consec. games 300 yds., career, 24—old 12, Jim McMahon, BYU.

8. TD passes, 3 yrs., 86—old 83, Jim McMahon, BYU, 1978, 80-81.
9. TD passes, career, 121—old 84, Jim McMahon, BYU, 1977-81.
10. Consec. games TD pass, 35—old 22, Steve Young, BYU 1982-83.
11. Yards by a soph., 4,560—old 4,322, Scott Mitchell, Utah, 1988.
12. Games 300 yds., season, 12 twice—old 11, Jim McMahon, BYU.
13. Consec. games 300 yds., season, 12—old 11, Jim McMahon, BYU.
14. Consec. games 200 yds., career, 27—old 22 Steve Young, BYU.
15. Games 300 yds., career, 33—old 17 Jim McMahon, BYU, 1977-81.
16. Games 400 yds., career 12.
17. Yds. gained/attempt (min. 237 attempts),11.07—old 10.27, Jim McMahon, BYU, 1980.
18. Yrds./comp. (min. 205 comp.), 17.2—old 16.1, Jim McMahon, BYU, 1980.
19. TDs, freshman and sophomore seasons 45 (13 & 32)—old 40, Bernie Kosar, Miami (Fla.), 1983 (15 & 25).
20. Yards per attempt, career, 9.82—old 9.00, Jim McMahon, BYU, 1977-81.
21. TD passes at conclusion of junior year, 86.
22. Yards, career, 15,031—old 11,425, Todd Santos, SDSU, 1984-87.
23. Games 200 yds., career, 38—old 30, Kevin Sweeney, Brian McClure, Doug Flutie
24. Yards vs. one opponent (N. Mexico), 1,495—old 1,482, Doug Flutie vs. Penn St.
25. Yards/game vs. one opponent (N. Mexico), 373.8—old 370.5, Doug Flutie, Boston College.
26. Completions, 3 yrs., 875—old 787, Brian McClure, Bowling Green.
27. Attempts, 3 yrs., 1,377—old 1,251, Brian McClure, Bowling Green.

28. Attempts, 4 yrs., 1,530—old 1,484 Todd Santos, SDSU, 1984-87.
29. Completions, 4 yrs., 958—old 910 Todd Santos, SDSU, 1984-87.
30. Yards/game, career, 326.8—old 309.7 Mike Perez, San Jose St., 1986-87.
31. Yds./completion, career, 15.68—old 15.62, Doug Flutie, Boston Collge, 1981-84.
32. Highest pass efficiency, career, 162.7—old 156.9, Jim McMahon, BYU, 1977-81.

Passing tied (2)
1. Consec. games 200 yds, season, 12 twice—ties Robbie Bosco, BYU, 84 & 85.
2. Games 200 yds, season, 12 twice—ties Robbie Bosco, BYU, 84-85.

NCAA ALL-TIME RECORD LIST
(As of 1991 collegiate season)
Top 10 Career Total Offense Yards Per Game

Name	Years	Games	TDs	YPG
1. Ty Detmer, Brigham Young	1988-91	46	135	318.8
2. Mike Perez, San Jose State	1986-87	20	37	309.1
3. Doug Gaynor, Long Beach St.	1984-85	22	45	305.0
4. Tony Eason, Illinois	1981-82	22	43	299.5
5. David Klingler, Houston	1988-91	32	93	291.5
6. Steve Young, Brigham Young	1981-83	31	74	284.4
7. Doug Flutie, Boston College	1981-84	42	74	269.5
8. Brent Snyder, Utah State	1987-88	22	43	268.9
9. Larry Egger, Utah	1985-86	22	42	256.9
10. Jim Plunkett, Stanford	1968-70	31	62	254.4

NCAA ALL-TIME RECORD LIST
(As of 1991 collegiate season)
Top 10 Total Offense Career Yards

Name	Years	Plays	Yards	YPP
1. Ty Detmer, Brigham Young	1988-91	1,795	14,665	8.17
2. Doug Flutie, Boston College	1981-84	1,558	11,317	7.26
3. Todd Santos, San Diego St.	1984-87	1,722	10,513	6.11
4. Kevin Sweeney, Fresno St.	1984-87	1,722	10,252	6.03
5. Brian McClure, Bowling Green	1982-85	1,630	9,774	6.00
6. Jim McMahon, Brigham Young	1977-81	1,325	9,723	7.34
7. Terrance Jones, Tulane	1985-88	1,620	9,445	5.83
8. David Klingler, Houston	1988-91	1,431	9,327	6.52
9. T.J. Rubley, Tulsa	1987-91	1,541	9,080	5.89
10. John Elway, Stanford	1979-82	1,505	9,070	6.03

NCAA ALL-TIME RECORD LIST
(As of 1991 collegiate season)
Top 10 Career Passing Efficiency

Name	Years	Att	Cmp	%	Pts
1. Ty Detmer, Brigham Young	88-91	1,530	958	.626	162.7
2. Jim McMahon, Brigham Young	81-83	1,060	653	.616	156.9
3. Steve Young, Brigham Young	81-83	906	592	.652	149.8
4. Robbie Bosco, Brigham Young	83-85	997	638	.640	149.4
5. Chuck Long, Iowa	81-85	1,072	692	.646	147.8
6. Andre Ware, Houston	87-89	1,074	660	.615	143.3
7. Doug Gaynor, Long Beach St.	84-85	837	569	.680	141.8
8. Dan McGwire, Iowa, SDSU	86-90	973	575	.591	140.0
9. John Elway, Stanford	79-82	1,246	744	.621	139.3
10. David Klingler, Houston	88-91	1,261	726	.576	138.2

NCAA ALL-TIME RECORD LIST
(As of 1991 collegiate season)
Top 10 Career Passing Yards

Name	Years	Att	Cmp	Int	Yds	TDs
1. Ty Detmer, Brigham Young	88-91	1,530	958	65	15,031	121
2. Todd Santos, San Diego St.	84-87	1,484	910	57	11,425	70
3. Kevin Sweeny, Fresno State	82-86	1,336	731	48	10,623	66
4. Doug Flutie, Boston College	81-84	1,270	677	54	10,578	67
5. Brian McClure, Bwlg Green	82-85	1,427	900	58	10,280	63
6. Ben Bennett, Duke	80-83	1,375	820	57	9,614	55
7. Jim McMahon, Brigham Young	77-81	1,060	653	34	9,536	84
8. Todd Ellis, South Carolina	86-89	1,266	704	56	9,519	49
9. David Klingler, Houston	88-91	1,261	726	38	9,430	91
10. Erik Wilhelm, Oregon State	85-88	1,480	870	61	9,393	52

DETMER STATISTICS

Freshman Year
1988—Pass Efficiency: 138.0

Opponent	Carries	Gain	Loss	Net	TD	Att.	Comp.	HI	Yards	TD	%	Plays	TO	S
Wyoming	6	7	46	-39	0	26	9	4	133	1	.346	32	94	5
Texas	0	0	0	0	0	3	2	0	64	1	.667	3	64	0
UTEP	4	0	13	-13	0	14	8	0	82	1	.571	18	69	1
Utah State	2	5	5	0	0	5	3	0	13	0	.600	7	13	0
Colorado St.	0	0	0	0	0	0	0	0	0	0	.000	0	0	0
TCU							—DID NOT PLAY—							
Hawaii	1	0	4	-4	0	10	5	0	132	1	.500	11	128	0
New Mexico	5	13	24	-11	0	35	24	0	333	5	.686	40	322	2
San Diego St.	7	27	14	13	0	13	6	1	45	0	.462	20	58	2
Air Force							—DID NOT PLAY—							
Utah	2	32	5	27	0	20	10	2	238	2	.500	22	265	1
Miami	5	3	19	-16	0	27	16	3	212	2	.593	32	196	3
*Colorado	4	4	14	-10	0	17	11	0	129	1	.647	21	119	1
88-TOTALS:	32	87	130	-43	0	153	83	10	1252	13	.542	185	1209	14

*Bowl statistics are not included in season or career totals

Carries = Carries; Gain = Yards Gained on carries; Loss = Yards lost on carries; Net = Net between gain and loss on carries
TD = Carries resulting in touchdowns; Att = Passes Attempted; Comp = Passes Completed; HI = Passes intercepted (Had Intercepted)
Yards = Total passing Yards; TD = Passes completed for touchdowns; % = Percentage of passes completed
Plays = Total number of plays in game; TO = Total offense for game; S = Sacks

DETMER STATISTICS

Sophmore Year
1989—Pass Efficiency: 175.5

Opponent	Carries	Gain	Loss	Net	TD	Att.	Comp.	HI	Yards	TD	%	Plays	TO	S
New Mexico	11	35	56	-21	1	29	19	0	323	0	.655	40	302	4
Wash. St.	10	59	34	25	0	53	34	3	537	4	.642	63	562	5
Navy	2	6	5	1	0	35	26	0	353	2	.743	37	354	0
Utah St.	6	24	12	12	0	35	18	2	330	3	.514	41	342	2
Wyoming	10	6	55	-49	0	30	16	0	337	2	.533	40	288	6
Colorado St.	7	11	27	-16	1	38	20	2	338	3	.526	45	322	3
UTEP	4	9	12	-3	1	28	22	2	426	3	.786	32	423	0
Hawaii	13	12	89	-77	0	35	24	2	427	1	.686	48	350	10
Oregon	11	37	45	-8	0	47	29	2	470	3	.617	58	462	4
Air Force	5	5	17	-12	0	27	16	1	334	4	.593	32	322	2
Utah	2	10	0	10	1	22	18	0	358	4	.818	24	368	0
San Diego St.	4	21	10	11	2	33	23	1	327	3	.697	37	338	1
*Penn State	8	29	11	18	2	59	42	2	576	2	.712	67	594	4
89-TOTALS	85	235	362	-127	6	412	265	15	4560	32	.643	497	4433	37

*Bowl statistics are not included in season or career totals

Carries = Carries; Gain = Yards Gained on carries; Loss = Yards lost on carries; Net = Net between gain and loss on carries
TD = Carries resulting in touchdowns; Att = Passes Attempted; Comp = Passes Completed; HI = Passes intercepted (Had Intercepted)
Yards = Total passing Yards; TD = Passes completed for touchdowns; % = Percentage of passes completed
Plays = Total number of plays in game; TO = Total offense for game; S = Sacks

DETMER STATISTICS

Junior Year
1990—Pass Efficiency: 155.9

Opponent	Carries	Gain	Loss	Net	TD	Att.	Comp.	HI	Yards	TD	%	Plays	TO	S
UTEP	4	6	9	-3	2	46	33	2	387	1	.717	50	384	1
Miami	11	32	25	7	0	54	38	1	406	3	.704	65	413	2
Washingtn St.	10	22	31	-9	0	50	32	2	448	5	.640	60	439	4
San Diego St.	3	0	30	-30	0	38	26	0	514	3	.684	41	484	1
Oregon	6	0	56	-56	0	57	33	5	442	2	.579	63	386	3
Colorado St.	3	8	5	3	0	38	26	3	316	4	.684	41	319	1
New Mexico	5	7	35	-28	1	41	26	2	464	5	.634	46	436	2
Air Force	2	7	1	6	0	43	30	0	397	3	.698	45	403	0
Wyoming	11	26	42	-16	0	50	35	2	484	2	.700	61	468	4
Utah	4	12	19	-7	0	50	28	2	451	5	.560	54	444	2
Utah State	6	4	43	-39	0	50	32	5	560	5	.640	56	521	3
Hawaii	8	21	15	6	1	45	22	4	319	3	.489	53	325	3
*Texas A&M	4	18	45	-27	0	23	11	1	120	1	.478	27	93	2
90-TOTALS	73	145	311	-166	4	562	361	28	5188	41	.656	635	5022	26

*Bowl statistics are not included in season or career totals

Carries = Carries; Gain = Yards Gained on carries; Loss = Yards lost on carries; Net = Net between gain and loss on carries
TD = Carries resulting in touchdowns; Att = Passes Attempted; Comp = Passes Completed; HI = Passes intercepted (Had Intercepted)
Yards = Total passing Yards; TD = Passes completed for touchdowns; % = Percentage of passes completed
Plays = Total number of plays in game; TO = Total offense for game; S = Sacks

DETMER STATISTICS

Senior Year
1991—Pass Efficiency: 168.5 (Career 162.7)

Opponent	Carries	Gain	Loss	Net	TD	Att.	Comp.	HI	Yards	TD	%	Plays	TO	S
Florida St.	6	18	28	-10	0	32	19	1	229	2	.594	38	219	3
UCLA	10	34	42	-8	0	46	29	2	377	2	.630	56	369	5
Penn St.	9	8	46	-38	0	26	8	1	158	1	.308	35	120	6
Air Force	8	61	19	42	0	30	20	1	340	2	.667	38	382	2
Utah St.	5	17	9	8	1	30	21	0	329	2	.700	35	337	1
UTEP	10	8	63	-55	0	39	22	2	378	3	.564	49	323	5
Hawaii	8	19	23	-4	0	20	14	0	225	3	.700	28	221	2
New Mexico	4	35	0	35	0	39	24	0	375	4	.615	43	410	0
Colorado St.	1	0	6	-6	0	28	23	0	337	3	.821	29	331	1
Wyoming	3	8	0	8	2	30	20	0	306	2	.667	33	314	0
San Diego St.	8	50	46	4	0	54	31	3	599	6	.574	62	603	4
Utah	3	14	20	-6	1	29	18	2	378	5	.655	32	372	2
*Iowa	8	12	37	-25	0	44	29	1	350	2	.659	52	325	4
91-TOTALS	75	272	302	-30	4	403	249	12	4031	35	.618	478	4001	31
Career	265	739	1105	-366	14	1530	958	65	15031	121	.626	1795	14665	

*Bowl statistics are not included in season or career totals

Carries = Carries; Gain = Yards Gained on carries; Loss = Yards lost on carries; Net = Net between gain and loss on carries
TD = Carries resulting in touchdowns; Att = Passes Attempted; Comp = Passes Completed; HI = Passes intercepted (Had Intercepted)
Yards = Total passing Yards; TD = Passes completed for touchdowns; % = Percentage of passes completed
Plays = Total number of plays in game; TO = Total offense for game; S = Sacks

Quarterback Ty Detmer
6-0, 175

"Dan Marino never had that kind of night against us. Detmer is a great one. He smells of confidence. He has a great feel for the field and was not confused at anything we threw at him. We threw a lot of things at Detmer that a lot of good quarterbacks have not handled well over the years and were confused with. He wasn't."
—Penn State Coach Joe Paterno

"He had me running around like a chicken with my head cut off. We didn't play that bad, Detmer is just that good. He knows all of the options, all the outs. I used up everything I had, but we didn't stop him."
—Penn State linebacker Andre Collins

"I've seen a lot of passers, but this guy—I've never seen one like him. He reads defenses like nobody else I've ever seen at such an early age. I've never seen one go to the second receiver as young as he does. And I've never seen anyone go to the right receiver at the right time as often as he does."
—Vince Dooley, Georgia Athletic Director and former football coach

"Detmer is a tremendous quarterback—as hot as any quarterback in the country right now. He did a great job of reading the defenses, adjusting when we were blitzing. He's very elusive. He's a quarterback of great promise for the future."
—Air Force Coach Fisher DeBerry

253

"He's (Detmer) a great quarterback and should get a lot of credit for the victory. He's very cool and calm under pressure. There were times when I was rushing when a lot of quarterbacks would have given up and taken the sack, but he stood in there and got the ball off."
—J. T. Tokish, Air Force defensive tackle

Detmer's certainly as good as I've seen."
—Colorado State Coach Earle Bruce

"I can see why he's (Detmer) leading the nation. He reads coverages well and picks up blitzes well."
—Craig Jerslid, Colorado State strong safety

"Detmer is playing awfully well, about as well as any quarterback I've seen this year."
—Utah State Coach Chuck Shelton

"He's the best-kept secret in America."
—CBS Sportscaster Brent Musburger (11/10/89)

"He is the best quarterback in the country. I know that is a lot to say, but I firmly believe that. He's as good at executing, reading and knowing what to do as anybody I've seen. He just makes good decisions. He knows what he's doing. He's a great football player. You couldn't make a mold and have a guy turn out any better than Ty. He is humble, yet possesses great leadership ability and is well-liked by his teammates. He has innate skill on the football field. We're glad he's back for two years."
—BYU Coach LaVell Edwards

"He reads coverages and gets rid of the ball when he's supposed to; that's why he's very difficult to sack. He's a very, very accurate thrower. He's a great quarterback, no question about it."
—**Coach Dennis Erickson, Miami**

"He is the best at making something good out of bad that I've ever been around. Detmer had to make great plays, and he did."
—**Coach Al Luginbill, San Diego State**

"He has such command of the field. He's an excellent runner, too. He'd be an excellent wishbone quarterback. We were just unable to get pressure on him all day. I certainly think we helped him in his chance to win the Heisman Trophy. Heck, maybe he'll even send us a thank-you."
—**Coach Fisher DeBerry, Air Force Academy**

"Ty Detmer is the best college impact player I've ever seen. I've played against three or four Heisman Trophy candidates, but if you were starting a team who would you want? Detmer. I think he should win it. I think he deserves it. He does more for a football team than anyone I've seen in a long time. He has great scrambling ability, great sense of where the heat is. You know who he reminds me of—and Detmer may have a better arm—is Fran Tarkenton."
—**Paul Roach, Wyoming**

"He's (Detmer) just better than I ever thought he was."
—**Mitch Donahue, Wyoming defensive tackle**

"I'll say the same thing about Ty I said about Jim McMahon when he left college. He'll lead someone to the Super Bowl. Ty will be an outstanding NFL quarterback at some point. He'll go somewhere and wind up playing. Whoever was starting will miss a game...and never get his job back. That's how I see it happening."
—LaVell Edwards

"You see a lot of great athletes come out as quarterbacks. But you don't see a kid with his knowledge and experience come out very often."
—Steve Young, San Francisco '49er quarterback

"You ask me if Ty Detmer's 15,000 yard career passing mark will be surpassed and I've been around too long to say it never will. But if you ask if I bet it will be passed, I would say it will be a long, long, long time. What Detmer did in just one of his seasons was remarkable. What he did overall was fantastic."
—Jim Van Valkenburg, NCAA Statistics

"Ty's ability to read defenses and his decision-making made him the ideal trigger man in our offense. He was a playmaker and with him on the field it was like having another coach."
—Norm Chow, BYU quarterback coach

"Ty set a benchmark in college football which may never be equalled. He is the most decorated college football player who ever played the game. His 15,000 yards could stand for decades. No journalist has covered Ty more consistently and in more depth than Dick Harmon."
—Assistant BYU football coach Claude Bassett

"Nobody ever had a game like that against us. Ty Detmer is fantastic. He can pick you apart if you give him the time. If you blitz him, he'll find the open man and burn you."
—Joe Paterno, head coach, Penn State

"If Ty Detmer were a baseball pitcher he'd have all the pitches. He is the best quarterback in college football. That one touchdown pass he threw against us was an impossible pass to make. I don't know how he completed it."
—Bobby Bowden, head coach, Florida State

"He reads defenses like nobody I've seen at such an early age."
—Ex-Georgia coach Vince Dooley

"The first glimpse I had of what Ty Detmer was all about was during a game in 1988 when he was just a freshman. After one play Ty chewed out receiver Chuck Cutler for running the wrong route. Here was this rookie standing toe to toe with a team captain telling Cutler where he messed up. That took moxey. Dick Harmon has captured the essence of Ty Detmer and provided insight into many more instances of who this remarkable athlete is."
—Paul James, KSL radio

Comment on Green Bay Packers drafting Ty Detmer in the ninth round: "That is the greatest bargain since the brinks train robbery."
—Lavell Edwards

"Tough, courageous, lots of perseverance... Ty Detmer is a heck of a quarterback on and off the field."

—Roger Staubach, Heisman Trophy winner and former NFL quarterback

"Ty is a fearless, confident, and composed competitor. The players follow him and respect him, not only for his athletic ability, but even more for his character.

"Ty has a field sense much like Jim McMahon. He knows everything that is happening on the field, offensively and defensively, where everyone is on the field, and where they're supposed be.

"Ty told one of our receivers, who was supposed to run a route over the middle, 'If you're scared, don't play!' That's Ty Detmer."

—Lance Reynolds, BYU running back coach

"Even with all the success that has come to him, Ty is still very coachable and down-to-earth. His competitive and winning attitude are an inspiration to everyone around him."

—Robbie Bosco, Quarterback coach and former BYU quarterback.

"I've set my personal goal... when I grow up, I want to be just like Ty."

—Sonny Detmer, Father and former coach

Quotes from Texas
High School Coaches

Gaylard Fenley, Alamo Heights:
Obviously, he has done a lot for Southwest High School. He's the one who makes their offense go. He's a good athlete. He plays basketball and baseball and ran the hurdles in the district track meet. He also was the only golfer that Southwest had in the district golf tournament.

Troy Burch, New Braunfels Canyon:
Probably the best thing I can say about Detmer is that he is the very best at reading defenses that I've seen during my coaching career. He has a coolness about him that you don't see in a high school junior.

You don't ordinarily see that in a high school quarterback, period. He not only read our blitzes but our secondary coverages as well. I don't know if he's the best quarterback who has played around here, but he would have to be one of the best. We expect to see him again next year. He has great receivers and he uses his two running backs very well, too.

Ron House, Edgewood:
He's got a great future. He is one of the best young quarterbacks I've ever seen. He's very deceptive. He sets up real quick and it doesn't look like it because he's a big kid. He is one of the best quarterbacks I've seen around here.

When we played them this year, I felt he did an awfully good job of reading the defense and picking up the man who was open. He does that better than anybody I've seen.

I guess that comes from always being a quarterback. he's been playing quarterback since he was a little kid. He picks a defense apart. I hate to see what he's going to do next year.

259

Bill Farrar, South San West:
I think he's one of the best passing quarterbacks around. I really don't know what his limitations are. He's calm, cool and can thread the needle. I really don't see how Southwest can be stopped. The whole key to their offense is Ty Detmer and his ability to throw under pressure. He is very good at reading defenses.

There aren't too many quarterbacks like him around on the high school level. When you run into a quarterback like him, especially with the blocking and receivers Southwest has, boy, you don't know how to stop him.

You can play fantastic defense but he's going to beat you because he's going to hit his receivers as soon as they break off their route, He has the ability to get the ball there as soon as the receiver makes his break.

Bill Murphy, Laredo Cigarroa:
We saw him early in the year and he was good at that time. In my opinion, he probably is the best passing quarterback I've ever seen in Texas. He has a great touch on the ball and has all the tools to be a good passer.

Besides a great touch on the ball, he has a great sense of timing and a great sense of what's going on around him. He's real cool. First of all, he gets a real deep drop. It's probably one of the deepest for a high school quarterback.

Jay Patterson, Medina Valley:
The thing I noticed about Ty is that he reads defenses very well. There aren't too many high school quarterbacks that confident in reading defenses. He picks up secondary receivers very well when you blitz him. He puts the ball on the mark and can hit a receiver on the dead run.

First Round Draft Pick QBs vs. Washington State

Name	C-A-I	%	TD	Yds	Eff.	Pts	YPA	Score
Jeff George Illinois, '89	16-43-1	.370	1	82	42.21	7	1.90	L 41-07
Andrew Ware Houston, '88	8-18-2	.286	0	42	27.00	0	1.50	L 21-00
Todd Marinovich So. Ca. '89	27-41-1	.654	1	268	123.23	18	6.54	W 18-17
Troy Aikman UCLA, '88	27-44-12	.614	1	325	126.43	30	7.40	L 34-30
Totals/Avg	78-156-8	.500	3	717	*72.90	55	*4.40	
Ty Detmer Vs. Washington State, 1989-90								
1989	34-53-4	.640	3	537	162.66	41	10.13	L 46-41
1990	32-50-2	.640	5	448	164.26	45	8.96	W 50-36
Totals/Avg	66-103-6	.641	8	985	*162.44	86	*9.56	

Detmer had 53 fewer passing attempts, yet completed just 12 less passes than the combined total of the four other quarter backs. He had 168 more yards than the combined total yardage of the four.

*Average of all four quarterbacks' totals vs. average of Detmer's two games.